GERIATRIC MONOLOGUES

Geriatric Monologues
Some Smiles and Frowns From the Road Most Travel

A Reading Theater Play
offered in One Act and Two Act formats
with extensive as-produced notes from
the original Two Act presentation

Written by
Jim R. Rogers

ISBN: 978-0-9895042-8-7

*Information about purchasing
and royalties contact
jimrogers@sc.rr.com*

Jim R. Rogers
POB 14028
Surfside Beach, SC 29587

Prose Presss
Pawleys Island, SC
prosencons@live.com

Contents

5

This Reading Theater Play is based on the author's books of poetry *Starts and Stops Along the Way and Looking Around.* It is a thematic collection of poems and narratives about the trials and tribulations, smiles and giggles, regrets and regards, successes and failures, memories of sad times, and those of joy, of love… all from the road most travel as told by those long on the journey.

This play book is dedicated to the two
who made it happen with love and care
and constant support.
My friend and book guru Bob O'Brien
and my life wife, Sally Z. Hare.
I am grateful.

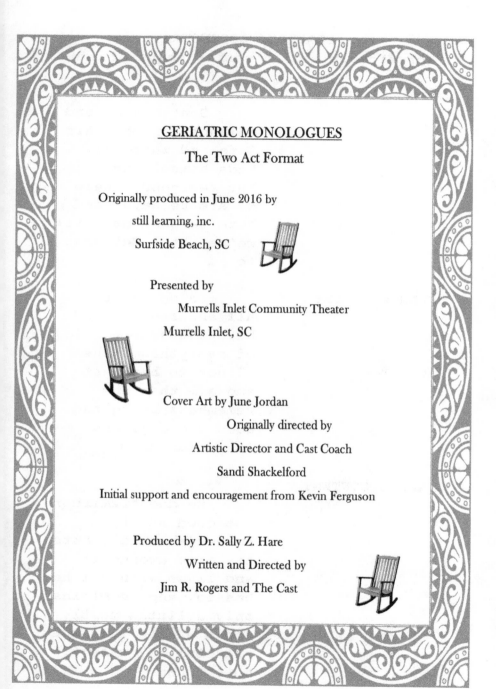

GERIATRIC MONOLOGUES

The Two Act Format

Originally produced in June 2016 by

still learning, inc.

Surfside Beach, SC

Presented by

Murrells Inlet Community Theater

Murrells Inlet, SC

Cover Art by June Jordan

Originally directed by

Artistic Director and Cast Coach

Sandi Shackelford

Initial support and encouragement from Kevin Ferguson

Produced by Dr. Sally Z. Hare

Written and Directed by

Jim R. Rogers and The Cast

PLAYERS/MESSENGERS
(preferably all in senior years of age)

BERNARD FIND

> Sentimental and melancholy about his life and where he finds himself in it, but resigned. Here we are he says, and here we will be until we're not. Get used to it.

MELANIE MEMORY

> In spite of all she sees around her, the growing old of everything, she clings to her past and all that she remembers being the good ole days and longs for them.

CHARLIE CONTENT

> He does remember the good stuff, smiles about it, puts his arms around it and lives with all he has to, and complains only a little mostly about what's lost but grateful for what he's found.

ROBERT RANT

Wonders where it all went and who took it from him! Can't settle for what is, what will be and instead talks about all that's wrong and how it could have been different if he had been in charge.

JANE DOMORE

Miss Do-gooder who wants to do more. The professional volunteer and cheerleader nudging all her aging allies to get up and get going. So what! We can't change it! Stay busy, fill the mind, move the butt.

JAMES LAMENT

He wants to change it all. None of it suits him and he knows in his heart that maybe he got it all wrong and he can't go back. He can only move forward, if he chooses, and he's working on it.

SANDRA FINI

> Digs deeper for
> thoughts and beliefs
> to comfort her. Of
> course it's going to
> end, but how and when
> and why are there
> questions and no one,
> even though they
> tried with loving
> care, has given her
> any answers. Are
> there any?

(SETTING)

The final porch of life where self-made
philosophers act as messengers and rock
to the rhythm and the beats that formed
their lives and lead them to a place
of sharing and remembering, composing
acapella poetic operettas of what's to
come for most.

(TIME)
The last years.

(NOTES FROM THE ORIGINAL PRODUCTION)

Lighting and minimal stage props are
involved. Singles with pools of light or
follow spots could be used, with multiple
pools for highlighting several at a time.

There are seven very different rocking chairs on stage. Set as they might be on a large porch in conversational areas where seven friends get together to talk about the times in which they lived and are living. Actions could involve some choreography for rockers depending on physical abilities of cast members.

Options: Staged (theater) readings…. with stands…sitting with scripts, moving around with scripts…memorizing it all (tough for the original cast.)

The book on which this adaptation is based offers readers a chance to make notes to themselves on pages left blank at the end of each section of seven. There can be an offer of a similar opportunity to the members of the audience at an intermission (15 minutes) or in an after show Talk Back. Blank cards and pencils can be available with suggested questions to think about and write about can be displayed. The reflection time could be announced, or visually shown on stage. There could also be old vintage photos shown as back-drop for scene or section change.

There are seven Parts (scenes) to the play, the first four comprising the first act, and the last three the second act. In the original production, decorative vaudeville type Show Cards were used on an easel at the corner of the stage and each card is changed to denote the transition of the parts. How the cards are shown and by whom is completely optional. In the One Act format, they are displayed on a table after being set there by the player. No specific direction is given. Flexibility and choice are encouraged.

The Parts of the play were transitioned with lights fading to black and back up again with a designated actor changing the Parts Show Cards, then using an on-stage retro cassette player that this group has when they get together. (OPTIONAL) The player has seven 30-40-second musical selections that would have been popular in the younger days of the group, but are still fondly remembered and listened to often.

Blocking and/or cast staging depends on physical ability of the members. Originally, there were minimal entrances and exits (limited access and agility) and most action directions had to do with remaining in a sitting position or standing for a speech alone or joining in a grouping when the subject is similar. When interaction of the cast makes sense, it should happen, although most of the time the cast speaks directly to the audience.

AUTHOR'S NOTES FROM ORIGINAL PRODUCTION.

Since there are many parts of the dialogue where subject content connection is not vital to the narrative, permission is given, encouraged, to the producer/director to feel free to interchange speeches from the full Two Act format, to the modified One Act format and vice-versa. Time constraints are important but some speeches may be better suited to a player than others, and to a certain audience. For example, the "Don't cry for me dearest Tina..." in the Two Act, was inserted in the commercial premiere of the One Act format with some other speeches deleted for time.

The movement of the monologues is from realizing age is on its way, going through the stages of it, bouncing back and forth between taking the process lightly and falling into the pit of sadness over the inevitable. Effort is made to see, hear and feel that progression getting heavier as the monologues move toward the end but not forgetting hope; that there is still life until there isn't. Not a traditional play but rather dramatic readings mirroring the many and varied emotions that go with aging, these words are meant to inspire, encourage, console, comfort and offer some grins to folks who often don't have a lot to grin about.

Some plays are performed from rote
memory and some aren't. This one mostly
isn't. We are following that rare
tradition because it suits the material
and it suits us. Older brains find
memorization a considerable effort, so,
really...why bother? (From the desk of
the original Director)

Part 1

So This Is It?

When we start
becoming aware
that we are
getting old.

GERIATRIC MONOLOGUES

A Reading Theater Presentation
of a Two Act play

<u>So This Is It</u>

(CURTAIN, IF AVAILABLE)

(The Rocking Porch. Seven empty rockers
of diverse design and size are on an
empty stage (although props may be used
to help the porch setting look more
real and comfy.) They are arranged in
conversation areas as might be the case
on a real porch. As the lights come up
full, BERNARD FINE walks in briskly
goes to the cassette player, starts a
piece of music, goes to opposite side of
stage adlibbing to audience, i.e. "How
about a little mood music?" etc. is ok,
and changes Show Card from "Geriatric
Monologues: Some Smiles and Frowns From
the Road Most Travel." to "Part 1: So
This Is It!" He announces the card to
the audience, returns to the cassette
player, stops the music, then addresses
the audience while walking to what will
be HIS rocker.)

BERNARD
Who wants to be old?   (CHARLIE and
MELANIE enter), Not he! Not she! Not I!
(SANDRA, JANE, JAMES enter and meander
toward rockers)

JANE/CHARLIE
Not we!

MELANIE
But we are.

JAMES
So we are.

ALL
Yes, we are!!

ROBERT
(Entering in haste and irritated)
Leave me be! (He sits hard in his rocker
and talks soft) But don't leave me alone.

BERNARD
So, here we are, on the way to being old.

JAMES
Released from corporate structure,
mandates, orders, expectations.

MELANIE
Raising children.

ROBERT
Raising cain!

JANE
And all that required stuff of the early
years. What will it mean?

SANDRA

We don't know. We've never been here
before. Others have but that's them. Now
it's us.

CHARLIE

Set free to be younger, healthier, empty
nestier, for now.

BERNARD

Decisions still. But new. Like
rearranging the deck chairs on the
Titanic.

MELANIE

Where to go. Downsize. Upsize. Gated.
Apartment. Condo. Parent house out back.

ROBERT

Or attached!

JAMES

Retirement community. The village.
(UNPLEASANT) The dreaded facility with
nurses.

SANDRA

Real old folk yearn to stay.

ROBERT

Home values down. Once a second floor...
status. Now a pain in the rear.

BERNARD

Smart senior-friendly home.

JANE

Comfort is what we want. Something more than shelter.

MELANIE

Where we can be us. Where we have memories.

CHARLIE

Where we can age in place. Where we can be old folks AT home.

(All slowly move to their respective
rockers and either sit or stand beside
them. They are suddenly jerked into
attention by BERNARD)

BERNARD

Zip! Swoosh! Zing! Those are the sounds it made as it went by. It started slow enough, young eyes sparkling with discovery; finding the joy in it, wanting each day to last longer than the one before, especially summer. And they did drag sometimes, mostly when you wanted to date, to drive, to smoke, to drink, to be left alone. And then you are. How fast it goes now. Twice the speed of light. Hard not to fall off. Not what you thought. Not what you dreamed. Not where you wanted to be now. But here you are. So? Cares get more refined. Time is told in different ticks and tocks. No stones left to un-turn. Shirts and pants don't match and once I wore two different shoes. No one noticed.

(They are all quiet with some smiles and
head shaking in knowing agreement of the
reality)

JAMES
(Joins Bernard who remained standing)

You're not acting like yourself, they
said. I've never been who I am before,
so I don't know if I am myself or not.
The problem is that you don't know what
you want to be when you grow up until you
grow up and then it's most likely too
late to start. (Smiles knowingly) Unless
it's not!

ROBERT
AARP is our badge…to inform, advocate,
guide our paths away from ignorance with
dignity, respect…like 91% of us over 65
have at least one chronic condition.

JAMES
(Interjecting)
Thanks for that, AARP!

ROBERT
(Continuing)
And sell us really tacky mail-order
clothes…shoes that don't need lacing.
Sex aids! Because it's never too late!
And sticks with springs and claws for
reaching where our bodies won't go.

JANE

Calendar pages. One by one they come and go. They don't mean anything at all unless we want them to...in the mind, in the heart, in the desire, in the joy of being alive to turn another page.

MELANIE

Not much thought at the time about who our children would be. Not much effort to help them get there. Here. Maybe too late to do much now. Maybe not.

JANE

Maybe not.

JAMES

When we watched the playback of the Christmas video it hit me over the head like a ton of bricks. That was me!! I was the old man! While I wasn't looking, I had aged. I had not been unhappy really, and I had been healthy and I had been doing my work well and supported and loved, so how the hell did I get so old so fast! I knew it was time for me to actually do something with my life, fulfill my purpose, make a real difference, do something for god's sake or one morning I would wake up dead with the excuse that I had been too busy or I really didn't know what to do or how to do it...so I did something else.

SANDRA
(Getting out of rocker and
addressing the group)
How about reunions? Went to one...knew
none, until faces came through...wrinkles,
spots, sag, time...and there they were...
classmates again, shining, smiling,
faking, appearing... in spite of it.

CHARLIE
Stuff! From years. Stacks and layers from
room to room and paths, and detours to
bed. What to do? Where to go? Who wants
what's there...on the walls, in the halls,
shelves so full. Boxes now. What to do.
Out they go. Here I stay.

BERNARD
Which way. I could have done this or I
could have done that but not both. How
the hell do we choose?

ROBERT
We don't! It chooses us.

JAMES
(Rising, to audience)
Pick and choose. We have to do more of it
now. That's what aging offers. Can't do
it all any more, don't even try, only so
many hours, so many weeks, so many days
and nights to go. So many choices get
slimmed down to the few that we want to
do, be with the ones we want to be with,
hug only those who know we mean it, cut

the do list down to done. I've never done
that before. I'm giving up that never
ending one. Routines can go out, take
risks for once, be late sometimes but
be sorry, too, since we still respect
and want to get it back. They think
it's merely idle hours that we do, just
staring into space, half out of it, when
we're really just staring into past,
looking to tomorrows, to what's still
there. The ole noggin still works!! So
let's spend the time that's left the way
we want to spend it. We don't be rude
or sharp of tongue, we can stay polite
and caring, but we can be bold and not
ashamed to let the ones who count, count.
Just make sure they know it.

BERNARD
Talking along...and Bam! Can't think of the
next word. Stalled in mid-sentence while
they wait to see if I make it!

ALL
Yeah, right, happens to me

MELANIE
(Standing to audience)
Morning. First check obits. Who's there?
Who's not? Not me! Made it another day!
So many have so much... long details.
Everything they ever did... Awards, Honors,
Successes, No failures.(Just this one if
you can call it that.) wondering... now mine
won't be that much... very little really.

Less is more? Life is not measured by the length of the Obit. Is it?

ROBERT
(Stands to audience)
Here's a tribute to Jack Nicholson, 5 Easy Pieces.
She's everywhere. In the drug store. At Hardees and BoJangles. In the grocery deli. At the doc's office. She takes my movie ticket. At breakfast there are many. The hospital has a few. Airplanes too. Big box check-outs for sure. It seems to be just old folks. Males and females both. There must be a school she goes to to learn just how it goes. She means well, that's for sure, but I always want to say...unless you want to bed me, don't call me honey!

ALL
(ha, ha, and jest and agree, and then settle down to a silence...as JAMES moves toward center stage.)

JAMES
(Pontificating poetic.)
(He walks and talks or reads...as the lights slowly fade on the others, leaving JAMES alone in a forming pool of light.)

Old glory. Smiles, and happy times and much more than a lot, not encumbered. They rested there, reclined in the folds of my mind, knowing but not knowing that

someday they would stretch and unfurl
once again to wave in the winds of life.

It feels good to fly, to be exposed to
the elements, to sag one minute, only
to burst forth with currents of emotion
not allowed to be for fear of pain, for
fear of another loss, a loss of something
never had.

Notice the edges ... wear, starting to
tear, eating into the very heart of the
design across which stitches and patches
have been applied, holding it together
for yet another reveille and taps, hoping
for a longer day to separate the two...
and sunshine is best. It only fades the
colors. Flag bearer, flag bearer, feel
how soft I am, how thin I am, sometimes.
You as one so close can almost see clear
through. Saluted. Applauded. Honored.
Protected. Pitied. Extended. Retired.
Hang it on a flat wall in the den or frame
it behind glass. No more wind. No more
sunshine. Only pool and sometime parties
and pro bowls and empty TV. Occasionally
an admiring eye who sees what once was
there.

(He slowly walks to his rocker and sits,
        pleased with himself AS LIGHTS
                FADE TO BLACK.)

Part 2

Seems Like Yesterday

Remembering the
younger days of
plans and
expectations.

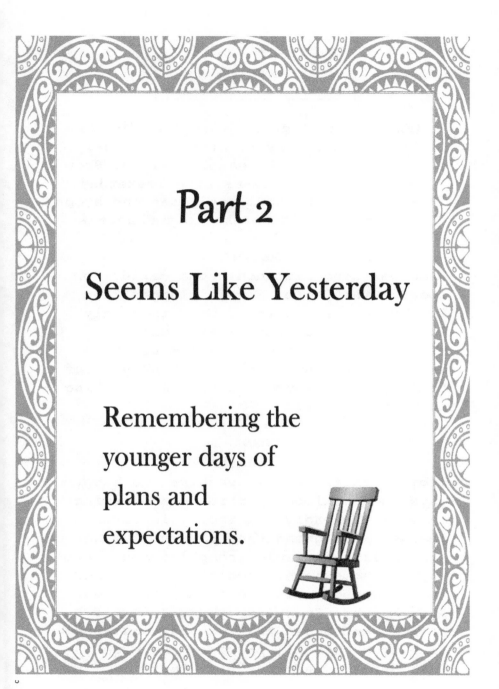

Part 2
Seems Like Yesterday

(From dark, lights up as Melanie goes
to cassette player, starts her music
selection, goes to easel, changes Show
Card to "Part 2: Seems Like Yesterday."
Reads it to the audience, goes and stops
the music, and speaks to audience.)

MELANIE
Remember long distance phone calls? How
special they were. How we planned them.
Looked forward to them. Used them only
for very special occasions. Amazing
miracle of the times. How I miss those…
and hand written notes of "thank you"…of
"hello, how are you? I've been thinking
about you a lot."

BERNARD
(Standing)
From birth there was sunshine and happy
days and Huckleberry friends and caring
parents, friendly neighbors, inspiring
teachers and grandstand cheers. The world
was small and simple, complications were
way off somewhere. Special and destined
to be somebody different than they had
ever known. Everybody thought it and he
took it and began the race that he knew
nothing about. Ill-prepared but eager,
full of hope, he took his steps.

Tomorrows became todays, they became the past, and what of the life?

CHARLIE
(Stands, joins BERNARD)
Out of the house I went... away from all that I knew, feeling the world like never before... eyes wide... heart ready... brain growing... each one, fresh, exciting, worrisome, then scary. Then too many... one, two, three more life teachers giving, getting some but not enough. One so odd and would not fit. One so bright, so right, so wrong. Maybe home was best. No way it's so... just go and go and GROW!

JAMES
(Stands, joins the others)
It was supposed to be simple, clear, direct, and even easy. But it just got complicated. There was no way a young and idealistic boy from a Norman Rockwell town could have prepared for what he got... On the Job training. Why do we wait so long before we start telling the truth? (PAUSE) Maybe it takes that long to find out what truth is?

ROBERT
Whatever I have is what I've got. No more. No less. It's mine. I worked hard, lived long, loved many, lost some, laughed a lot. And cried. Whatever I have, it's mine. Whatever it is.

MELANIE

Like FAMILY? FAMILY... Glue that holds us
together. Gets too hot and melts. And the
pieces fall apart, but stay sticky.

SANDRA
(Rising to group and audience)

When do you know it's time for a change?
Where does the idea first come from?
A distant spot of sail on the mind's
horizon gliding slowly toward you,
getting fuller and bigger and closer and
stronger as it sensitizes your knowing of
the wind.

JANE
(Rising to join SANDRA)
Or, does it grow like a seed in the
ground, getting larger and healthier
as its environment of need waters and
nurtures it to blossom and beautifully
lulls you into the notion that you had
better move from where you are. Sometime
soon.

ROBERT
(Rising to join the others)
Or maybe it starts as a mental cold sore,
causing just a hint of the pain that is
to come unless you do something, but of
course you don't know all that unless
you've gone through such change before,
and if you have, then why are you letting
yourself in for all that shit again?

MELANIE
(Rising to join others)
It could be that you are just sick and
tired of being sick and tired as the
12-steppers say. You could be just stuck
in a mud rut, adjusted to the goo and
slow movement, and not do anything but
stay stuck. Then, there's that classic
cliché when the pain of staying is worse
than the pain of leaving. That's when you
have to change. To do otherwise would be
totally foolish.

BERNARD
(Rising to join others)
And yet being foolish doesn't seem to
matter. When I am deep into dysfunctional
comfort, I don't care if I'm foolish or
not; I care about whether or not I am
happy. But, even then happiness is so
fleeting: One minute high, another low.
I always feel empty when I'm happy…and
guilty. It won't last long and there are
so many others who aren't. So, I don't
do anything.

JAMES
(Stays seated and reflective with
hint of kidding)
Well, they say that's a decision. You
know, it's just too much trouble. I
don't think I can change. Not if my life
depends on it. Maybe it does. Naa.
What's the big deal? In this case…I'm
just hot that's all and I need to cool

this room down. Now let's see. Is it up
to cool or down to cool? Never can get
that straight. Should I take a chance,
or wait for somebody who knows?   I think
I'll wait. For now. Maybe.

(The others chuckle and take their seats,
except JANE.)

JANE
Decades. So many. So many of us. So
many paths we took. So many stories to
tell. So much happened in our decades. So
many of us. So alike. So different.

ROBERT
So what!

BERNARD
Passion. Used to drive me. Got me up. To
go. To do.

(ROBERT interjecting OH YEAH!)
Got me up for that, too.

BERNARD
Knew I could energize when needed. Get
it done. Make 'em applaud. See how good I
am. Where has it gone? Away from me and
I can't seem to find it again and I had
nothing to say about it.

JANE
Oldies but goodies. We listened to music

that we loved, danced closely, whispered
stuff that came to be. Doing it still.
Loving it still. Now that we are Real
Oldies, Real Goodies.

JAMES
Afternoon and early evening nods come
and I can't stop them. Tired. Run down.
Bored. Exhausted. Snorts wake me! Ashamed
when I don't respond to a question,
react to a birdie, or participate in
conversation. (PAUSE) Is this the sleep
before the BIG sleep?
Oh...TRYOUTS!!

SANDRA
Little things you never thought to be
hard, are. Just getting out of a chair
without soreness, pain, grunting,
pushing, pulling, regretting, finally
accepting the limitations that come with
the territory.

BERNARD
Sitting in a room, crowded with interested
guests hanging onto the speaker's words
of wisdom. Except me. Hard to hear from
where I am- 6th row. Ashamed to cup my
hand over my ear. Both sure signs of age.

ROBERT
(Pleased with his add on)
And vanity!!

JAMES
(Rising and walk and talk)

Vanity? I still have that. Something else
I had. Dreams. I had a few of those.
Wanted to be a cowboy and ride horses and
shoot guns and kill bad guys and be the
hero of my life. I had to let go of that.
Wanted to be the quarterback, and make
touchdowns, and win exciting games, get
the girls and be a champion all-star.
I had to let go of that.
Wanted to be a great lover, with lots of
conquests, play the field for all it was
worth before finding the most beautiful wife
to be mine forever.I had to let go of that.
Wanted to be a Hollywood star, admired by
the world, with a fan club and magazine
covers and the most cheered acceptance
speech for Oscar.I had to let go of that
Wanted that perfect family, with that
perfect wife, perfect gender children, a
beautiful home in the best neighborhood,
driving the most expensive car on the
block.I had to let go of that.
Wanted a vacation home, on the lake in
the mountains, with an inboard motor
boat and a dock with water sports,
excellent restaurants near-by and envious
neighbors.I had to let go of that.
Instead I got to be a respected
accountant, an effective lineman, a shy
woman-magnet, the president of Kiwanis,
owner of a mortgage-free home in the nice
suburbs, after one divorce, a perfect

wife with intelligence and beauty, and
four unequaled children, two of each,
all college graduates…and I was voted
volunteer of the year when I was 70.

I hold on tight to all that.
   (As he sits, ALL gives approval with
"atta boy", "way to go", "good job," with
      some scattered applause.)

JANE
This I know for sure…sitting too long in
one place, feeling like the world has
passed you by and woe is you because
you're old, will push you deeper into the
pluff mud of nothing, into more nothing,
until you disappear! But doing something,
any something, will move you…activate
yourself, and one grows into more, then
many and many gets you going again.
What's that those shoe people say…Nike...

ROBERT
Just do it!!

JANE
Yeah, that's it…Just do it! They got it
right, alright.

BERNARD
Used to be just three channels, and
sometimes less…early morning, day time,
until midnight…cheap entertainment on the
tube. Now, Wow!! A vastland of choices,

twenty-four hours seven days, three-hundred-sixty-five. Everywhere you look, listen. So much there!

                    ROBERT
            (Another zinger for him)
              Not much there!!

            (ROBERT stands and continues)
Yeah, and what about all those remedies
for whatever ails us! All through that
vastland countless commercials telling us
who to be, how to be, when to be, what to
be...And the magical medicines...The best of
all! Helping us anew...but watch out for
"The Sides"... nausea, headaches, bloat,
weight loss,

(ALL others get it and join in with their
              own contributions)

                    SANDRA
              or gain...hives...

                    JAMES
              HBP...LBP...gout...

                   BERNARD
         depression...anxiety...mood swings...

                   CHARLIE
         lost wages...shortness of breath...

                     JANE
shortness...tallness...mother-in-law blues...

MELANIE
mass murder tendencies...Rose hater...
Terrorism Tactics...even death...
(Now, everybody jumps in with their own
creations of maladies to cure until it is
chaos of over-talk)

(ROBERT picks it back up and closes
it out as they all get a hoot and a
holler with their contributions and the
silliness of the pharmaceutical world
on TV)

ROBERT
Yeah, ok, whoa...And so on...and on and on.
Unbelievable!!! Not me! I'm sticking with
what I've got.

(With comments like "me too", "that's what
I think:...they all slowly move back toward
their rockers and settle back in.)

BERNARD
Aging they say is all in your head...
That's true except the parts that are in
your knees, your hips, your joints, and
assorted other parts, where aches and
pains hang out and greet you daily, just
to remind you and keep your head from
getting too lonely.

JANE
Along the way...many starts, many stops,
checking in to see what was there for me.

JAMES
Found and lost.

SANDRA
Lost and found...

ROBERT
People, Places

CHARLIE
Things, Feelings,

BERNARD
Ideas, Beliefs, Hopes,

MELANIE
Dreams, Realities,

ALL
Starts and stops along the way.

(LIGHTS OUT, THEN BACK UP AFTER
ABOUT 10 SECONDS.)

Part 3

Sit Down And
Stay Awhile

Reflecting on some
of the best times
relived and
remembered.

Part Three
Sit Down And Stay a While

(JANE goes to cassette player, starts
her music selection, then to SHOW CARDS
changing to "Part Three:Sit Down and Stay
A While." She announces to the audience,
then stops music and sits, inviting
CHARLIE to speak...)

JANE
It's all yours, Charlie.

CHARLIE
(Dragging his rocker closer to the edge
of stage making more intimate connection
with audience. He sits to begin.)

CHARLIE
I'd like to share with you a note I wrote
to my late wife. My life wife. We had
been married for four years at the time.
(Takes out folded letter, unfolds and
reads.)

"Hey, you. Love has not been a stranger
to me...I have known her. She embraced
my mother and me and my father in an
entirely different way. She showed me
her way with my brothers and cousins
and aunts and grandmother and friends,
although looking back, that may have been
something else.(Rising and pacing)

As I grew, she showed me more and let me
love a wife in a way that I could then.
There was care and caring but there was
always still me. Later, she introduced me
to passion and that was good. And then
came romance and then came otherness. Out
of nowhere, love matched me to another
who knew her in a different way, but a
way that made me feel...Loved. I finally
arrived at the ultimate love, I thought.
She gave two a connection and a bond
and that, too, was good.   And then
she changed course. Love redefined. She
became something else. Romance waned.
Passion cooled. Only care remained. And
otherness. Still.

"Confused and despondent. How could she
have changed to something else?

"And now I know. She changed to become.
Love has gently warmed her way deep
into a place I didn't know existed. She
has revealed a part of her that goes
way beyond anything imagined. She has
let me have this time with her very own
incarnation. She has given me herself.
She has given me you."

I found this as I was going thru her
letter box last month. She kept it for
47 years. I hope she took it out and
read it every now and then, to make up
for those years that I neglected to tell
her how much I loved her. I hope she did
that. (He drags rocker back and sits.)

SANDRA
(Remembering)

So sweet, Charlie. Makes me remember
Spooning. The greatest pleasures and
comforts of the day, any day, are those
when the last light is out, the dogs are
quiet, the nite lights are soft, and I
snuggle up and hold him gently firm, being
just where I want to be… then it's his
turn to hold me. Even better. What a fit!!

BERNARD
How about this one. Bubble Stuff. She
called him her "bubble stuff". He had
mixed emotions about it. When they were
alone, he blushed a bit, smiled, and he
wanted to rub up against her cat-like
and get whatever else she had. When
she used it in mixed company, even with
close family, he would give her a look
that said "that's private, "flush red, and
retreat to another room of conversation,
or busy himself in the kitchen. His
daughter thought it was cute and sweet.
She liked that finally someone actually
loved her dad. Like he deserved.

JANE
Finding joy was a daily discovery in
youth... except for the disappointments
that came…the hurt…the heartbreaks. Made
me strong and wise so today I can still
have joy…with the disappointments, the

hurt, the heartbreaks.

                    ROBERT
Temptations galore. Sitting there
staring…just asking us to take, eat,
drink, buy, speak, risk, try, go, stay,
feel, give, keep

                  ROBERT/JAMES
        (Do a give and take on these lines)

          JAMES Ignore.

          ROBERT Sure.

          JAMES Easy.

          ROBERT Not.

        JAMES Use wisdom.

          ROBERT Ha.

        JAMES Use will.

          ROBERT Ha. Ha.

                    MELANIE
        (Taking her time and getting
            close up to CHARLIE)

Will you remind me to tell them to fix the
overhead light in the car?

                    CHARLIE
Who's going to remind me?

                    MELANIE
Let's leave notes. Remember to do that.

                    BERNARD
You remember to do that. And remember to
remind me to remind you.

                    MELANIE
Ok. Ok. I forgot. You remembered.

                    CHARLIE
You forgot. I remembered.

                    MELANIE
Takes two of us to make a good one.

                    BERNARD
Difficult getting through the days,
feeling like no purpose. Tired of doing
stuff I don't really want to do. Tired
of going just to be going. Tired of
worrying about the kids and if they'll be
all right. Tired. Just tired. Then she
comes, I smile and want her, filled with
energy forgetting tired. That stuff comes
from another place!

                 JAMES/JANE
               (Alternate lines)

PDA. Public display of affection. PDA.
Private display of affection. Either is
fine with me. For me. For some, public

emotion varies... shy, shame, proud,
private, cute, sweet. Well, a little
hand-holding never hurt anybody. PDA
Private...? Well now that's another matter.
(Together) Our own.

CHARLIE
Many times, I'd say, closer please.
She'd say, I can't get any closer. I'd
say try. She did. And did.

ROBERT/JANE
(Rising, interacting, alternating lines.)

You'll tell me if I have food in my
beard? If you'll tell me I have spinach
on my tooth. If I talk too loud. If I
talk too much. If I repeat myself. If my
jokes aren't funny. If the blackheads
show. If the hairs need tweezers. If
I eat too fast. If I'm unkind. If I'm
fading fast. If I'm still pretty. If I'm
still a hunk? Oh, yes. Still. OK then.
We're fine.

SANDRA
(Rising, joins Robert/Jane)
Grandchildren come and go...like children,
leaving us behind. Their life. Their
choice. Like we did to them. But before
taking off, what pride, what angst,
what pain, what worry, what joy. What
memories!

JAMES
(Rising, joins others)
Our son told us today that he and family
would not join us for this holiday. They
see us all the time, so they are going
somewhere else to see someone else they
don't see so often. (Sarcastically) We
understand completely. Hello New Rationed
Parents!
(JAMES EXITS)

MELANIE
(Rising, joins others)
We did some things. A place where smiles
come easy. The couch is a teddy bear for
many. Finding comfort even in discord.
The place is safe enough for honest
words. The time together renews the bond.
The people there embrace you. There was a
hole now pushed way back, filled in with
growth that only time can give. Gifts
and food and care abound. That place we
nurture and get it from. How they long to
greet the roots. We made it strong and
holds us well.

(Three together.)
Home.

(All three exit randomly.)

SANDRA
(Slow and sad recounting)
One, two, three, four, five, six…The
monthly visits now. Agreed places where

we go together...hand in hand...But not in
step. We never were in step. Thank god
for that. But we were in love.

CHARLIE

Movies have always been favorites.
Saturday afternoon horse operas, cartoons,
shorts, classic features and most not.
Right through the many years to computer
generations of Avatars and Transformers
and walking dead zombies. So many movies
warped my sense of time. Pieces of lives
lived in scenes sewed together with
music, effects, and explosions created
unreal time lines, hiding the worst... the
days between are the hardest to take.

(CHARLIE EXITS)
(ALL EXIT leaving
SANDRA alone on stage.she has started to
nod off as the lights fade

Part 4

Whose Life Was It, Anyway!

Taking stock of some
of the disappointments
and dislikes that
accompany us
on the trip.

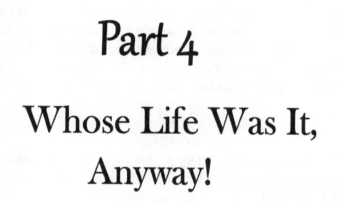

Part Four
(Whose Life Was It Anyway!!)

(Lights up as ROBERT enters, goes to cassette player, starts his music and does a little dance as he goes and changes show card to: "Part Four: Whose Life Was It Anyway!"He stops the music and startles SANDRA from her nap with...)

ROBERT

Irritations!!! (Says to wake SANDRA, then continues)...Irritations on the small stuff come more often and quicker. Impatience with an open drawer. Child-proof medicine bottles! Those ads inserted in magazines that have to be ripped out. How thin can they make paper anyway? Wasting time trying to turn a page. Why are there stickers on my apples?!! And remains of stickers on my gifts! On the front where they can be seen! The dirty dish in the sink. Stacks of stuff in the way...(Moving into sadness) The way she says no now... the way she never says yes. The way she rolls her eyes. The way we turn our backs, in bed. In life. (Sad, he sits)

BERNARD
(Entering)

So many times, I feel like screaming!
Unfair. Unjust. Rude. Ignorant.
Incompetent. Intolerant. Inconsiderate.
Mean. Hands tied. Mouth shut. Inside
heat... with nowhere to go.

JAMES
(Entering)

I knew this guy. He often envied those
who knew why they had been born. The
natural athlete, or explorers or teachers
who never even thought about being
anything else. They came to do a certain
job, and they did it, got very good at
it and were honored for having given
their all to the job or to others. He
could have gone in so many different
directions. He had some talent in many
areas...and choosing one, or even two,
proved to be melancholy to him now in his
last years. He often wondered if he had
gone in another direction, what would his
life have been like? If he had chosen to
pursue his first love, or even his second,
would it have made any difference in how
he felt now?

CHARLIE
(Enters joins other two)

I've had thoughts about it all. Maybe tell
her now that he has been dead for a year.
Cancer got him young. Been thinking about
it all and how dying early takes care of

any old age second guessing...and wondering
about what comes next...and whether we did
all we wanted to or... we bog down in the
misery of lost life and regrets. You know,
we should tell her this.

                    MELANIE
        (Who enters during CHARLIE speech)
No... Don't Tell Her. She knows.

                (RESPECTFUL PAUSE)

                    ROBERT
            (Getting up and happily
             changing the mood)

Hey, there were these two senior seniors
giving each other The Middle Finger in
the parking lot at the post office. Both
right. Both wrong. Drew quite a crowd
wondering... does it really matter? It sure
seemed to to them.

                    ROBERT
Well, listen...even the most intimate
friends never know about the sagging
balls in the toilet bowl water. (ALL do
double takes and smile widely) This is
the age when men make close friends of
urinals!

                    CHARLIE
Getting shorter was a surprise. Another
unexpected gift of aging!

ROBERT

And, honey-do lists!!! And our responses
to them...like...I'll get to that!!

JANE

I'll get to that, I'll get to that...

MELANIE

And, I'll get to that, to that, and that...

JAMES

I'll get to that, and I'll get to that,
too...

BERNARD

And I'll get to that, and that, and I'll
get to that!

(AFTER A BEAT, IN SYNC)

ALL

Pretty soon now!!!
(They all laugh at themselves
and settle in)

JANE

When you get old your body starts making
noise...starts talking to you...snap, crackle
and pop joints with vocal accompaniment...
Groans, moans, ows and ohs and a few
dammits. Hurts to move... to roll over
... to readjust. It hurts to change
positions... and opinions.

ROBERT

TV is my challenge. So much wrong and
I catch them at it! Yelling at the
stupidity of officials, of commercials.
Politicians. City officials. Did I say,
city officials. How about celebrities.
Did I say politicians. You think that's
good?! I think it stinks! No one cares.
I do.

BERNARD

Expand-a-waist pants! Genius. Fit like
a glove. Pride lost to bulge. Why not
expand-a-shirts? Now go to Goodwill
after 20 years. Button strain... then up a
larger size...on the cheap...breath- holding
time reduced 20%!

SANDRA

Senior ballet! One legged dancing...
not holding on... putting foot in pants,
underwear, panty-hose...finding balance,
being graceful... And fearful that it will
only get worse.

JANE
(Stands to deliver)
Reinventing ourselves is what we're
supposed to do.But I like me as I am.
They laugh at us. I know. I used to. We
wear strange clothes. They're old. Why
get new? They think we have bad taste.
They don't know that we just don't give
a shit. (PAUSE) We don't deserve it
all. Not all. But some for sure... Loud...

Self-centered... Selfish... Demanding... Don't
listen...Talk...A lot... About our lives...
Where we came from...What we did... Who we
were............... When we were.

JAME
(Joins JANE)

I used to laugh under my breath at the
way some old folks dressed. The leisure
suits, the matching nylon sweats with the
required stripe, or the twin tee shirts
with "I'm with stupid" printed on the
fronts, the Velcro strap shoes; the awful
taste in the matching of clothes...stripes
with checks, yellows with greens, greens
with blues. (My mother would croak!)
those dumb Henry Fonda On Golden Pond
hats...and the list is endless. I used to
think it was because they had no money
as well as no taste. They lived on a
fixed income and couldn't afford nice new
clothes and someone to advise them on
what to choose to wear. Now that I am
one of them, it's not money.

CHARLIE
(Finishing the thought)

It's what JANE just said...we don't care...
Some of us, that is. We aren't trying to
win another's heart, approval, blessing,
promotions, or anything. Why should
we care? Nobody pays us any attention
anyway. And if we really wanted them to,
then wearing this stuff is the surest

way to get their attention! What was it they used to tell us as young parents? Children need attention. If they don't get any, they will do something to get it. They would rather have negative attention than no attention at all. I think it works!!

ROBERT

The older I get, the more pissed off I get. It's no wonder old people get cranky with age. They see the end… they didn't get it all done… they didn't do anything they wanted to do much less everything they wanted to do. No time to start over. Trying to contribute….. Get disrespect… demeaned…discouraged. Pissed off! Like never before! I saw this poster recently of a lovely lady and her quote…"the older I get, the more people can kiss my ass!"

(MELANIE shouts ROBERT!!! Chastising as others feign horror! He takes a long breath and continues)

I'll tell you what bothers me! People who park in no parking, handicapped, wrong lane, wrong way, take up two parking spaces, biggest SUV on the block. People in movies talking loud at wrong times, putting their feet, sometimes bare feet on the back of the seats in front of them, leaving during the credits, blocking the view of others. Rude! Inconsiderate! Hard to tolerate rudeness. It's all about that for me. Pissed off. Again.

(ROBERT EXITS)

BERNARD

Sagging comes slowly but it comes. What was here, moved to there. Changing waist, other parts, too. Not seen but felt. Hell NO to T shirts, and all tight fitting anythings. Avoiding mirrors, reflective windows, anything that will show you to yourself!

CHARLIE

Directions. They say men won't ask for them. It's true. When I was young, I never did even getting lost for hours. Didn't want anyone to know I couldn't read a map...especially her...I could follow a sign...became dependent on signage... love that word signage. Poor signage, confusing signage, non-existent signage. When it is there, it's too late, or too small, or too faded. Signage is my new trigger word...a mad, angry trigger word. When I lose my way, I blame signage. I didn't read it right. It's my way of staying out of trouble. Blame something else.

JANE

Educate me? I don't want to know all
that stuff that will make me happier,
healthier, richer, wiser, skinnier,
smarter, social. I just want to be
Me. The real me. Hair growing where it
shouldn't... not growing where it should.
You know, hair today, gone tomorrow! Skin
gets thin...letting through those dark
places, the red, black, blue road maps
that were hiding there all along.

JAMES

All the money went to someone. Not me.
And now I sit wishing, regretting,
wondering, mad as hell, sad, too, and
not knowing what's next. Plans I had
derailed. Accidents. Fate. Illness.
Injury. Things happen. Unintentional
detours along the way. Plans changed.
There's no turning back. I can rewind and
look at it... pause and reflect on it. But
it's done. Can't change what was. Can
change what might be!

(JAMES EXITS)

SANDRA

There is no bottom to the depth of pain
we feel when there is loss. Moms. Dads.
Brothers. Sisters. Friends...But the worst,
by far the deepest pain...loss of your
child.

(RESPECTFUL PAUSE)

BERNARD

For a while I bitch, I moan, I complain
until I see a young man in a wheelchair
driving it with his chin and then I
realize how lucky I am...for a while

JANE

I whine, I lament, I yell unfair! until I
see a man with cerebral palsy painfully
inching his way down the sidewalk greeting
people with an awkward smile, and then I
realize how lucky I am...for a while.

CHARLIE

I get depressed, I become desperate,
I panic until I see a homeless woman
shivering among her cart full of worldly
possessions in a dark alley, and then I
realize how lucky I am... for a while.

SANDRA

I see frail, I see fear, I see no hope in
places where it all lives...in the eyes of
the old people filed away like discarded
papers that were once important.

MELANIE

What does it take to be permanently
grateful? Being a homeless, wheel-chair
moving victim of cerebral palsy and
becoming frail, fearful and hopeless?

ALL
I hope not.
(Respectful pause)

BERNARD

You know what!? I am tired of doing it. (OFF STAGE ROBERT YELLS YOU ARE?!!) (BERNARD reacts) Not that. We still do that. Some people don't think it works after 50. It does!! (A smile) What I'm tired of is pinching pennies. Writing monthly checks. Waiting for a real person on the phone. Waiting for the kids to call. Waiting for them to get a life! A thank-you note. From anybody!! Brushing teeth. Fixing my hair. Picking out what to wear. Taking pills. Doctors' appointments. Procedures Required. Social time. Bridge. Walking at the mall. Shopping. Golf. Drinking... Drinking. Not remembering... what's good.

(BERNARD EXITS)

MELANIE

Yeah, about picking our clothes. Comfort not style... Except to impress the others at the dragged-to socials, human service meetings, worships, weddings, funerals... a lot of those. So few look. Fewer care.

JANE

Can't talk about Hemorrhoids, Gout, Gas, Pimples, Flatulence, Psoriasis, Operations, Procedures, Children, Politics, Religion, Savings, Stock market, Neighbors, In-laws. But We do.

(JANE EXITS)

MELANIE

Growing apart it's called now. Growing together it should be. Could be. What have we become? Where is what we were? Along the way, the disconnect that we vowed would not be us. And here we are... together but apart... wondering, grieving what was. Hoping for something else... something that was. Again.

(MELANIE EXITS)

SANDRA

Mom chose Family Dollar Sweats. Gave her Bloomingdale blouses that stayed in the boxes... still the sweats. Why Mom? Easier. Finding, Choosing, Maintaining, Cold wash, No iron, three colors black, grey, and navy blue. Soft. Comfy. We were frustrated, bewildered.   Now we know. How smart she was. Now it's us... just nicer sweats. More colors.

(AUTHOR'S NOTE. IN THE ORIGINAL PRODUCTION, THE ROLE OF SANDRA WAS PLAYED BY AN 86-YEAR-OLD WHO WAS NOT VERY MOBILE, HAVING TO USE A CANE, SO WE DECIDED TO MAKE IT EASY ON HER AND KEEP HER SEATED THROUGHOUT. THIS LED TO THE BLOCKING OF STAGE BEING EMPTY OF EVERYONE BUT HER AND CHARLIE AS SHE FINISHED HER SPEECH. SHE NOTICES THAT SHE AND CHARLIE ARE ALONE, AND AD LIBS, "WHERE DID EVERYBODY GO??? CHARLIE REPLIES, "MAYBE TAKING A BREAK?... TO WHICH SANDRA LOOKS AT THE AUDIENCE AND

SAYS SOMETHING LIKE 'SOUNDS LIKE A GOOD
IDEA TO ME...WHY DON'T WE ALL TAKE A BREAK...
WHILE CHARLIE CHANGES THE SHOW CARD TO
"INTERMISSION, 15 MINUTES PLEASE.")

(CURTAIN)
INTERMISSION: HOUSE LIGHTS UP, STAGE
LIGHTS DOWN.
HOUSE MUSIC IN THE MEMORIES MODE.

Part 5

OK.
Now What?

Doing inventory on
how we are thinking
and what we're
going to do with
what we have.

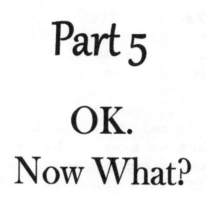

ACT II

Part Five

OK. Now What?

(As stage lights up
JAMES enters assisting SANDRA to her
rocker. adlibbing some chit chat as he
goes to cassette player, selects music.)

SANDRA
We all have our beliefs, don't we?
Practicing what we preach. Or not. So
many ways from so many places. Baskin-
Robbins flavors. It works most of the
time. Some think everybody else is wrong.
We all have the same goals... Heaven not
hell. Will we get where? Up to each.

JANE
(Entering)
Home work. In youth... chores, self,
clothes, room, bed, trash. School...home
work... More school...Home work... Job... Home
work. Life... Home work... Living, teaching,
growing, failing, falling, moving on, Our
own Home... More Work. Home work. Still.

CHARLIE
(Entering)
Time. It's been going on now for quite a
while, and I think I have learned some

64

things. Here's one. I don't waste as
much time as I used to. The process
of getting to depression and coming
out again is shorter. I can go to the
suicide mode and up to euphoria almost
immediately without messing around with
all that stuff in between.

MELANIE
(Entering)
Brick By Brick I build my wall… Ten
feet wide and twice as tall. Yes, I
wonder when they say, "That Wall is it
protecting you, or is it in your way?"

BERNARD
(Entering)
Self Help. Book shelves lined with
volumes… soul-searching philosophy…
simple and deeper poetry…for-sale
psychology from infomercials. A lot has
helped a little… a little has helped a
lot. A storehouse of searching, a library
of life. Along with others I've needed
all the help I could get to face the
unexpected firing squad. In it all I made
a find… the best single aid for grief,
loss, depression, frustration, confusion,
rejection, desperation, anger, hurt,
loneliness and all of the more, is to
have a little money in the bank.

SANDRA

Oh, I wish!!! I saw this on TV the other day. Something called Anthropology Navigator. Not sure if it's real but it made sense to me. Pilots, sailors and some hard headed husbands use it, too. Dead Reckoning. Explained by them as, to know where you are, you have to know where you've been. What it looked like, felt like, what it sounded like, who you were when, who you wanted to be. Then, you know if you've arrived.

JAMES

Well, I'm not so sure I've arrived yet... still working on it. (To Audience) Do you see me? Raise your hand if you see me...good...so many people don't see us old folks, do they?...I guess it takes one to see one.

It's hard not being who I was, but now it's so. I still am some, at least the parts that count. Some things don't and it's a good thing since hair is gone, muscle is less, get up and go is missing, joints need oil. Age is sneaky, you know it's back there lurking, waiting, all of a sudden, overnight there it is in the mirror, in others' eyes; it's the disappear potion and it works as you are no longer seen. No one takes you seriously. Old stories are just that and they don't count for much except to you.

Only a few regrets and only because of
sadness and pain you may have caused and
you have no idea about what's next; how
could you really? How could anybody? No
one has been there to tell it, to share
it, so you live each hour like the last
and mull it over and try not to hurt
again. Or we might end up on the line
somewhere believing that what has been was
a cruel joke or maybe an extraordinary
privilege. Of course. It's Both.

JANE
(Enthusiastic with hope)

Good Morning! I love the way a new
day feels. Those few moments when
yesterday's memories are slept into a
docile file for later. When rest gives
birth to new eyes that see a life with
energy and hope and a chance to try
again.

ROBERT
(Entering)

Hey, listen up! This is good. When I
started getting less busy, I became less
focused and driven. I didn't know how to
handle non hectic to-do time, and I would
forget stuff, 'cause I wasn't pressured
to remember. I would put off stuff, what's
the big deal...like the one I hate most,
paying by due dates. Then getting angry
when they charge the late fee. I still do
it. All the time. I'm in charge here.

MELANIE

Staying so long keeps so much stuck in
place. Pictures on walls. Nicks and
knacks on tables. Shelves crowding.
Closets full of never-worn favorites. No
room for more. Stuff accumulates over
time. Easy to see the floors, the doors,
how they show wear. But a slight movement
brings discomfort. Dogs bark. Even the
dust feels at home.

CHARLIE

As age creeps up on us, we become even
less concerned about our appearance.
Some of us anyway. We wear old clothes...
worrying about not spending that money
we may need for older age, and not to
burden the children and spouses. We have
nothing to gain by looking great, no
woman's hand to win, no job to compete
for, no seeking approval from others
'cause we're invisible to them, and the
young folks say look at that old fart/
ess with stripes and checks and pants
too short and tights not right and no-
style dress and hair a mess. And we just
smile. (long pause then bursting with)
WHO inspires us?!!

ALL
We do!!!!

ROBERT

Experience counts for something. For a while. Then it doesn't matter. Wrong experience! Not new! No E experience! Not up to date! Too slow! Too deliberate! Too much trouble! Still… Experience counts for something. It's ours.

BERNARD

I remember the day when that movie Flags of Our Fathers opened. I went on a rainy afternoon and it took my breath away. I didn't cry only because I stopped myself. And, as almost always, I was the last to leave the theater. I even stayed longer than usual as the lights eased on and the ushers flowed into the aisles, wielding their brooms and pans as they pulled the trash barrels behind them, attacking the mess that was just made mostly by senior citizens who had just seen Clint Eastwood's version of another mess, made by roughly the same generation. Generations often leave messes for the next ones to clean up. Have you noticed? Can we change that?

JAMES

I'm not as good as I thought I was...not as smart, not as special. I don't know what happened. Hard to admit we don't know it all, isn't it? Mother had drawers too stuffed to open. Why, mom? Not smart. Doesn't even make sense. Now you should see my drawers. If I could open them.

SANDRA

My hectic busy life is slowing down now.
My plan, as I have the time to think
often actually clearly, is to think
clearly. When time slows down, that's
when all the memories can come rushing
in. I am learning that there are many
more people than I who are more special
than I or who have probably suffered the
same haunting thoughts as I; that they,
too, were special and had a special
contribution to make in their lives and
wonder if it's too late.

JANE

No news is good news. Better than what
we see, hear, day after day after day.
Printed. Television. Radio. Painting
pictures of how bad it is, how bad it's
going to be… and no slowing down! So no
more news for me. I'll make my own, thank
you.

BERNARD

(Stands, moves downstage center)
Epiphany on the roof. Due to age, I
had to change the way I do things. No
longer strength, athleticism. Balance
now has to be. Planning, not taking
risks, taking breaks, using my brain and
staying focused… like not stepping on the
electrical cord and watching my feet slip
out from under me and rolling me off the
roof's edge smashing to the ground in one

large grunt with something broken that
will send me to the emergency room and
her into a dither. While I was creating
this new approach to living longer and
taking great pride in my discovery, and
losing my focus on the task, I stepped on
the electrical cord. Nope. I did not slip
down. Worse. I allowed myself a couple
of well-phrased ouch words loud enough
for the preacher in his yard next door to
hear, who responded to my Jesus Christ!
with Praise the Lord! And I heard her
coming. So much for that.

MELANIE
It's building. The complexity of it all
overwhelms me and paralyzes my brain. A
global community and so flat we can see it
all at one time. Too much to take in. It
freezes me in place.

CHARLIE
Timing. Reflexes waning, surprising.
Reaching for my red wine glass and
missing. Oops.

JANE
Old people are problems. We hear that. Of
course we are. One of our entitlements.
Should we be? We can be more the
solution. Nobody thinks to ask. Don't
wait. Tell them! Speak up! Risk it.
What do we have to lose?

SANDRA

Dogs. Einstein and Eleanor Roosevelt.
Not kidding. Their names, really. On
the daily walk as long as the journey
is underway, high spirits and jaunty.
But when they sense that we are about to
end it, return home, spirits fall and a
meandering delay sets in. As soon as we
sense the journey beginning to end, we
slip into depression, despair, rather
than enjoying to the fullest the time
on the we have left, one more sniff of
what's there.

ROBERT

Can't do it. Can't stop. Can't try.
Can't go. Get angry. No! Get really
angry! Mad! Pissed off! That might help.
Who? I say to people all the time...I know
I'm Right! How could this be wrong? Why
can't everybody be like me? Why can't
everybody be just like me? Mr. Perfect.
Then we wouldn't have any problems. (To
audience) Do I hear you smiling???

BERNARD

All my life there was this feeling way
down deep inside me that I was special.
All my life I felt that there was
something unique I was supposed to do.
All my life I found myself out of step
pretty much most of the time. All my life
I kept looking and listening for the
guidance, the direction, the way. All
my life I wondered how it would happen,

when it would happen and how I would
handle it. All my life it seemed to be
around the next corner. Hold on a little
while longer and you'll find it. All my
life the place I thought I was to be
wasn't the place for long enough to be
the final place. Here's where I made my
mistake. I actually believed what I was
told... that what I ended up choosing to
be, mattered. As we age we find that with
rare exceptions the rank and file common
man has little to do with what happens in
the world. Very little at all. But we do
have something to do with what happens in
our hearts. That's pretty special to me.

MELANIE
We start out small, inch by inch, pound
by pound we go, we grow into life
expecting good, happy, success. And
we get some, maybe lots. Maybe just a
little, if any at all.

ALL
(Alternately)

JANE- We embrace.

ROBERT- We push away.

CHARLIE- We look ahead.

SANDRA- We remember.

JAMES-We give. We take.

BERNARD-
We cry. We laugh.
And in it all we learn!

ALL
All life long!

JAMES
(Rising)
There are days I feel like I am waking
up after a long sleep. Now that I am
slowing down my brain activity and my
physical to-do list, there is more time
for me to see things I haven't noticed
in a long time, or never did, or thought
they were too menial to dwell on at the
time. I find myself seeing people, places,
and things…behaviors for the first time.

These are things I know… we all have
feelings of wanting recognition, approval,
applause. Adults and children alike need
involvement, engagement, inclusion,
interest, care… and if we don't get it,
we become sad, disappointed, resentful,
angry, uncooperative, and we act out in
many ways.

ROBERT
(Quickly rises and joins)
Like…ranting!? I've tried that. Done
it a lot. It always seems to end with
no results, but rather regrets over
embarrassing those around me and myself.
I want so hard to be Atticus Finch,

the first one, not the second one!   I
want to be emotionally mature,
conversationally brilliant, effective in
my convictions and persuasion efforts. (a
beat) I think I missed that boat.

BERNARD

Just because I am one, I don't have to
be one. An old person.   I'm not gonna be
one.   I refuse to be one. I don't like
what I see and I don't want to look like
them!

JAMES

Well, good luck with that! This is what
happens to us old folks as we realize
that we are going to die. Not sooner or
later, but sooner than later. We see it
beginning to lift its head yonder on the
horizon and it scares the hell out of
some of us. We're not ready to go yet.
We still have some fish to fry. We want
to see the grands grow up and prove that
generations do improve with each cycle.
We want to see if there is something
we can do to change it all and make it
better. Not only our lives past, but the
lives of the future old people who, as
young folks now, have no idea what's ahead
of them. You know what? Neither do I!

BERNARD

Yeah, all of us can say that. We don't
have crystal balls, but this I know
for sure…because we have less and less

say-so, or any power, or any sense of accomplishment or achievement...we do a whole lot of criticizing. Gives us artificial power, a manufactured coping skill to deal with failure or a sense of it at least or makes us feel that we know better. For a while there, as I unconsciously began to feel the pull of time gone and not complete, I started to criticize everything...I mean everything. Well, not her, even though she did do some stuff that drove me crazy, but with her, I bit the bullet. I didn't want to sound like a cantankerous old curmudgeon.

ROBERT

Yeah... I criticized the highway construction, a natural target. I didn't think they knew what they were doing. Why did they do this this way instead of that? Just didn't make sense. The on-and-off ramps were stupid and the way the DOT patched the roads was a joke. And the town crews, forget about it! I even criticized the new football stadium they were building at our university. It went up impressively but I just knew that they hadn't measured right. The playing field didn't look like it was 100 yards. It couldn't be. I actually laughed at myself for that. That's when I knew I was getting better...healthier. more hopeful...finding center and clarity. I think they call that "aging into wisdom." I hope so. I could sure use a little wisdom about now.

JANE

Maybe that's what's happening to me. The
first faint colors of my own mortality
have begun to glow around the outer
defenses of my living. Barely visible
now, I know they are there. Breathing
down my neck. Mostly they are shades of
foreboding gray. Not those fifty shades,
either...did you see that movie?

BERNARD
(interjecting)
Twice.

JANE

Oh, really! Well, is that wisdom?? Don't
think so! My grey is just one color...
dark...but I have to say...sometimes and
getting more often, it turns into many
pastels, and they are pleasing and even
inviting. And they will get brighter and
closer. And when that happens, I wonder
what I'll do?

SANDRA

Wisdom. That was something I did not
have much of early on. It was my normal
state of urgency. I have lived most of
my life with a long list of do's... and I
was damned good at getting stuff done.
I was raised to believe that you are
your work, and your achievements are the
shining stars of success in our world. I
had a work ethic so big I almost choked
on it. One of many positives handed down

to me by my Dad. Character. That was
his big thing. He was the most honest
man I ever knew. He worked hard his
entire adult life, finally living a few
years with his camellias and azaleas
before cancer got him at 61. I can't
cheat. I can't lie. Well, I can't
out and out lie. Little whites and
omissions, yeah, but they don't count in
today's world. They counted to my dad,
though.

CHARLIE

I feel guilty just sitting on the couch
and not having much to do anymore. I
feel that I have been given some unique
talents...at times I even considered myself
a renaissance man, but I believe you have
to be really outstanding at at least one
thing and pretty good at a lot of others
to qualify for that label. Maybe next
time. People tell me to stop feeling
guilty. They tell me to relax and enjoy
my last years to the fullest. I have
worked and worked hard for over 50 years,
and you would think that all of those
years I worked like other red blooded
American boys would have been enough.
So now I should just quit? Sure. Clint
Eastwood was doing his best work in his
70's. Now in his 80's and he's still at
it. I'm not gonna just sit around and
fade away, I'll tell you that right now!!

BERNARD

It's interesting what happens to us as we find ourselves with more time. Today, I didn't feel stress and pressures of taking care of the to-do list items, since there are few left on the list these days. So a lot of them fell through the cracks. And next month they will bite me in the ass.

ROBERT

At what point do I stop saying gee whiz, golly, oh my, I'm sorry if I caused you to misbehave...that you approach life differently than I...like those cutting people off in traffic, no signal, jumping in line, insurance companies not paying for procedures. Medicare mess, rude and incompetent clerks, politicians who don't get it. No follow up on calls, or activity. No return calls. Consideration. Polite. Basic manners. Teen-age cave men and women. Parents so caught up in their own mess, have no time, no desire, no clue about children. What I want to say is WHAT IS WRONG WITH YOU?!!!! How could you possibly think that is the way to act? Wouldn't help. Would it?

MELANIE

I have time to stop and talk with neighbors without feeling like I have to hurry and get on to whatever is next. I had time to go through the dry cereal

inventory, sorting out the old stuff
and putting the keepers into attractive
plastic containers, and I even tore off
the box top so we would know what dwelled
therein. Why do we do that? Find ways
to spend more time on frivolous tasks.

JANE

Maybe to help us feel a sense of
accomplishment, like we really are doing
something useful. Something we can
actually complete. I know that's why I
like to work in the yard, now. I used
to hate it, because I was too busy doing
other more important stuff.   You know.

CHARLIE

Yeah, I know. I used to pour my diet
coke kinda like I did parenting...fast and
on the run. And the coke always foamed
over leaving a mess for me to clean up
and then pour some more. Now, I have
more time. I do the slow pour. I stand
there pouring till the glass is full and
no foam or mess to clean up.
(Looks to audience and smiles) Smart!

LIGHTS DOWN FAST.

Part 6

My Time Has Passed

Accepting that we are
where we are and
how we are
dealing with it.

Part Six

My Time Has Passed

SANDRA
(Goes to the cassette player and starts
her selection as she picks up a basket
with small water bottles to pass out to
the group. But, she is stopped by groans
and moans of disapproval of music which
is too old... Silver Threads Among the Gold
old.   She returns and stops the music
with comments from the group, i.e. "I
thought you liked that old stuff...too old
for you, huh?" etc. as she offers waters
from basket and stops at the easel to
change the show card to "Part Six, My
Time Has Passed."
Then addresses the audience.)

SANDRA
(Walks back toward her rocker and sits
after lines.)

Volunteer. That's what we do a lot, and
we do it well. They need us. They love...
us... or they don't. They want us to help.
And, we do, too. Them. And Us.

JAMES
(Rising and to audience)
Something so mundane... Becoming so
important. Today, I polished my shoes.
My black ones, then my brown ones, buffed

my suede ones, new strings in my New
Balance all-purpose. Took my time and
did a good job. Didn't feel rushed to
get on to something else… polishing my
shoes was the something else. It had
been such a long time since I had done
it myself. Most times had them done by
the shoe shop. Stuff done by others. You
know, we busy people living life like
we're supposed to, fast, quick, always
in a hurry, just touching the surface of
things, too often forgetting value. Like
how important it was to have an unhurried
conversation with my son.

(Looks down) Nice shoes?
(Looks back up) Lost son.

ROBERT

I cry over what should be. I cry over
what could be. I cry over what is. I
also cry over what is. I sometimes laugh.
(Leans over close to JANE, who has closed
her eyes in thought, and says it louder
to wake her) I said, SOMETIMES I LAUGH!

JANE
(Coming alive!)

I'm not dead! I'm only resting. Waiting
to see which way I go next. New work.
New friends. New place. New peace. Dead?
Retired? No. Hell, no! Just resting.

MELANIE

Still doing the things I like. Going
where I can. Now there is more. More time
to do and go and be. More of others. More
of me.

CHARLIE

Who Served? Who served, we ask. It's a
pride cry for those who did. The big
WW two and several after. Some called
to. Some wanted to. Most Came Home.
Different. Too many did not come home at
all. Will we always war? Will we always
have to? Glory in winning with loss may
make way for the Next one.

JANE
(Stands with gusto)
We matter! Just when I thought I knew it
all, I didn't. Just when I thought I was
tall, I came up short. Just when I was
on top, I fell. Just when I was loved, I
lost. Just when I gave up, I got up. We
matter!

SANDRA

So, here I am. An old person. We all
are or are on the way. I have heard from
lots of sources that we are now in the
elder ranks…a position in life, I, for
one, accept. Because now, when someone
asks me to do something, I say, sorry,
elders don't do. We advise, we consult,
we point. We point things out…like, she
doesn't look 60 to me…more like 80! Or,

don't go anywhere with him, he drives
like a mad man, and he'll hit on you!!!
and we even point out some more serious
observations, like

MELANIE
(Stands, delivers and sits)
A.   That place in the darkness when the
lights come on.

CHARLIE
(Stands, speaks, then sits)
B.   He lost his strengths trying to
improve his weaknesses.

JANE (Stands and sits)
C.   That thud on the roof, it's a limb
from a tree. Got tired of hanging on, so
it just let go.

BERNARD
(Stands and sits)
D.   We point to leaves, falling gently
from trees, floating,taking their time, a
choice to let go with dignity.

SANDRA
So, now, as the elders we are and as
elders in our gained wisdom, we have all
the answers, you know. We feel it's our
obligation to share those answers with
you, some of them at least. Ones that
always worked best for us...like Huh?!!!

(CHARLIE)
You asking me?

(BERNARD)
Beats me dude.

(MELANIE)
I haven't a clue.

(JANE)
What are you talking about?

(JAMES)
How the hell should I know?

(CHARLIE)
Damn good question.

(MELANIE)
It's a mystery to me.

(ROBERT)
As De Niro would say...You talkin' to me?

(JANE in mystery)
Who ever knows, really?

(BERNARD)
Run that by me again.

(ROBERT)
Go ask your mother...your grandmother!

SANDRA
(concluding)
So, this ELDER wisdom ain't what it's
cracked up to be, is it? We are all
still learning.

BERNARD

We are all still learning. But some of
us learned too late, like those who have
gone under. Gone under. Good words for
the awfulness of a small business owner
losing her/his investment, savings,
relationships, credit, pride, security,
dream. So many in our lifetime... Gone
under. Pure sadness. I went under - once
was enough.

JAMES
(Stands reflective)

There's a picture of me holding my
18-month-old-son in my arms at the beach
on vacation and we were both in our
bathing suits and I was comforting this
sandy child who was obviously in some
sort of toddler distress. The picture
is one of many on my screen saver and
every time I see it, I dwell on it for
as long as I can...thinking, wondering
how different things would be now if I
could only go back to that time and start
again.

CHARLIE
(Joins JAMES)

When we start reflecting on our lives,
what we did and didn't do, what regrets
we have and what we would have done
differently had we had the chance, we
can either nose dive into depression and
wallow there until we slowly deteriorate
into nothing, or we can see the past

for what it was when we made choices, decisions, took roads we thought were best, making them on the knowledge and information we had at the time. Turns out some of that knowledge was incomplete, made complete only in the living of life over a life time, and the information was tainted by others who were also traveling on roads that were decided incorrectly for them.

JAMES

Either way we have to deal with the oncoming end. Some of us want to live it out no matter what the quality of life, since we are always teachers and learners even in death, and there are reasons for being here until we're not. Others of us want only to end the pain and despair that we feel and that we most likely will cause our loved ones left to take care of us and our dis-arrayed life. That's when we think if we should cleverly end it all.

ROBERT
(Stands and joins)

Hey, no, man…when you begin to spend 10 or 20 percent of your day thinking about how you could off yourself so nobody will know that you did, so the insurance will be paid, then we are wasting the precious little time we have left.

MELANIE
(Stands and joins)
Don't you think we are here to grow together, to mutate, to meld, to mesh into one human race...one in love, in care, in belief, in thought, in word, in deed and in spirit. Then we will be one with the creator...the universal energy that has split us all apart like a big bang to see if and when we will ever find our way back to wholeness.

SANDRA
(Seated and wise. Others look)
Or we could just be meant to be a diverse hodge-podge of humanity trying to figure it out dealing with all the crap it brings just being here. Who knows? We're just waiting to see.

(They ALL sit)

JANE
Waiting. For what? We use that excuse all the time...waiting till we lose weight. Feel better. Better time. I'll miss my show. Too much. Wrong day. Trouble. Tired. Angry. Sad. Depressed. Too late. Do it Now... Don't wait ...could be too late.

MELANIE
When you have nothing to do and it doesn't bother you, it's hard to find something you want to do. We criticize. Easy to do. So hard to take.

CHARLIE

So much to do. So much to still learn. So
much noise of knowledge. And pressures to
catch up from outside. Inside. Knowledge
gone wild! Overwhelm! and exhaustion!
Love my Naps!!

JAMES

Paralyzed in memories. Stuck in the past.
Nothing but fear of what's not there, of
what's not known. What am I going
to do today? Nothing. I've already done
that.

JANE
(Stands and delivers)

Skin thins. Turns into crepe paper.
Wrinkles wrinkle. Get deeper and
multiply. Feet unsure. Slightly now.
Minor bumps. But big ones may come...and
falls. Joints ache. Ears strain to hear.
Eyes squint to see. Teeth turn colors,
if they stay. Gait slows down. Thinking
takes longer. Uncle Sam's meds arrive.
Walkers and chairs that lift and... things
that say Old. How can it be? My self
still here! My heart still young! Life
still full! And ready for more!

ROBERT
(Stands and joins)

Me, too. Ready for more. Been ready!
I took the less traveled path. No one
there knew what they were doing, although
brave. Took the most traveled path... not

many knew there either. We keep guessing.
Keep trying. There might be an answer.
Do I need Will? To avoid the stuff
that could cut my life shorter. Will,
motivation to do what I know to do. I
can't find it. Where's will. I've lost
will!! What else you got?

BERNARD
(Stands and joins)
There's always anger. Deal with it,
Can't stuff it. It will go somewhere
else...inside...outside...all around. Can't
stay. Has to go. Has to be. How? Where?
When?...are the hard parts.

JAMES
(Stands and joins)
What I owe. What to give back? What?
Nothing. Got nothing, gave nothing.
Dissatisfied. Depressed. Slow death in
place. That's what's happening. What's
left? Just the alternative... See self
as a mess. Make that wake up call. Find
opportunities. Not problems. Find value.
Find purpose. Now's the time! What we
have already done doesn't really matter
anymore. What we have left to do, does!
There are things that we can do that we
should have already done, and now we can!!

CHARLIE
(Stands and joins group)
How about luck? What's luck got to do with
it? Is there any such thing? Luck be a
lady. Lucky break. Lucky me. Lucky you.
Luck smiled on her. Lucky they got to
where they were going before... Some people
got it. Some people don't. Do you think
it's so? Answer me this...Does Luck Run Out?

All
(Standing interacting)
Who gets compliments anymore?

JAMES
Used to be, Handsome,

JANE
Pretty,

ROBERT
Virile,

SANDRA
Great shape

BERNARD
Movie star leading man,

MELANIE,
Leading woman,

CHARLIE
You wear that well

JANE
Such fashion.

MELANIE
Now we know when we hear one coming,
"Oh look at you, you look great"

SANDRA
They are just being nice

ROBERT
Just plain old horse pucky, not sincere

CHARLIE
But staying humble as we were taught,

JAMES
As before responding with

ALL
What? Oh, this old thing?

(FAST BLACKOUT)
(Players take seats)

Part 7

The Road Most Travel

Knowing that the road
is going to end, and
wondering how we
travel those
last miles.

Part Seven

The Road Most Travel

Lights up slowly
(BERNARD goes to cassette player
plays his selection, then walks to SHOW
CARDS and reads the card as he reveals
"Part Seven: The Road Most Travel" Stops
the music and delivers.)

BERNARD
The only way I can make it now day to
day is to believe that all of it, all...
everything that happens, the good and the
bad are parts of the larger picture, the
grand design, the ultimate truth, the
way, the final secret, the revelation of
divine purpose, the coming together of it
all as one. Otherwise I would have given
up long ago...when it all started seeming
too real, unfair, with no meaning and
downright hateful stuff going on! The
enormous pain and agony suffered by most
of humanity.

SANDRA
(Stands and joins)
What could possibly be the purpose? The
world is taught about the love a heavenly
father has for his children, and it has
become more and more difficult to see how
that love and our hate, agony, desperate
and mean lives could possibly coexist,

even if a divine all-powerful creator
makes it so. I'm feeling it. Thinking it
is not knowing it, but it does help me
better understand and accept and believe
but, I don't have to like it.

BERNARD
(Delivers and both sit.)
I don't think we're supposed to.

CHARLIE
(Facing the reality)
It's out there. One is waiting for me.
Looking to pounce on or in me and take me
away. Which one? So many could. No signs
yet. Many seeds sowed. Who my folks were.
What they had. What they didn't have.
What I did. What I did not do. All sets
it up. Doctors and meds stall it all... one
for this, one for that. One will break,
through. One will take me down. In sleep
is best, of course. Oh, when I think of
all the damage to lives other than mine,
please, god, not a reckless teenage driver.

MELANIE
(Stands and moves to JANE)
Best friends come and go. Only the right
ones stay. You (to JANE) are one. My best
one. Stay.

JANE/MELANIE
(JANE stands, playfully back and forth)

New best friends. Pharmacists.
Receptionists. Appointment makers.
Cashiers. Bag boys. Technicians.
Mechanics. Handy men. Docs. Nurses.
Walkers. Hired Help. Meds... all of them...
(Together) Stay!

ROBERT
One. Two. Three docs for me and then four
more. Enough! No more! How many doctors
do we need to say what we all know...
Well, you're just getting old. Oh great!
How much do I owe you for that, doc?

We don't know it until we get here... how
life is so short. Now we know to be
selective. Don't waste time with what
we have. Choose carefully. Don't diddle
daddle! Oh, and don't forget to ask that
doctor if you're healthy enough to not
diddle daddle!!!

(RESPECTFUL PAUSE)

SANDRA
Thinking of those who have gone before.
Missing some. Ashamed at not missing
others. Parents. Friends. Work mates.
Wives. Husband. Brothers. Sisters. Aunts
and uncles. Some cousins. So many...
waiting for one of them to tell me what's
next. I've heard nothing yet.

JAMES

When her mother was sick and on her way
out, she was there, day and night and
in between. Little things. Big things.
Silly things. Serious things. Clean and
dirty things. Holding hands... sharing
tears and memories of mostly good. Loving
dedication to pay back what she got. She
was called The Angel. When she's ready,
who will her angel be? Maybe me.

MELANIE

Friends no more. It's difficult to even
see him now. Where did he go? That guy
I knew disappeared into his anger. His
regrets. His losses. His sadness. And I
can't seem to bring him home.

BERNARD

Getting harder to remember to take all
those pills. Got a daily dose box. Didn't
help. Forgot where I put it. I wondered
if missing days of doses would kill me.
Nope I'm still here. And,
I'm gonna make the most of it...if it kills
me!!

ROBERT
(Stands and delivers)
All the time we hear it. Fixed income.
Tight budget. Simplify. Downsize. Next...
all that's left... a bag of potato chips
and a walk-in closet!   What you put in
is what you get out. Heard that baloney.
I put in years, get back months, if
that. Put in time. Get back less. Put

in dollars. Get back pennies. Put in love. Get back loss. What you put in is what you put in...what you get back? Up to you. (Sits, passing Jane on her way down stage)

JANE

I find myself going to school again almost every day learning how things got this way. Polite was how we were, at least most times to strangers, sometimes, even family. "Please Wait" was an apology for the line too long, the clerk engaged; The plea from a soldier going to war leaving his sweetheart behind, please wait for me. Delaying a question, please wait till I can answer. Please wait a moment, Please wait your turn, Please wait and see, use patience please.

Now, TVs, computers, smart phones, tech help on line. Electronic things are always telling us "Please Wait." For what? Who knows why? They've grown so large we can't get in when it's best for us to try. We pay the price to have it now but it comes when they are ready. Please Wait, they say with "Please" to make it nice, they think. Frustration. Annoyance, impatience, confusion is what they get. So, I'm using it all for training now for when time comes to claim me, your turn now, so I can say, sorry I'm not ready.

Please Wait.

MELANIE

She faded. We watched her. Not
understanding why she didn't get up… do
something. Get out. Enjoy life. It's
becoming clearer. We understand now.
Giving up. Giving in. Digging in. Staying
put. Don't want to. Don't need to. Why
should I? Won't matter. Leave me be… but
love me, no matter what?

CHARLIE

How we do it? Deal with it all? Stuff we
didn't expect? Depends on where we came
from, who was there, what it was like,
what they did, what we did, what we have…
Somebody. Dollars. Support. Community.
Who we have become. How we feel about who
we have become.

CAST

JAMES
Home. It's where the start is.

JANE
Place of love and care.

MELANIE
For growing and knowing.

BERNARD
Finding Becoming Leaving.

ROBERT
Visiting less and less.

SANDRA
Making another home.

CHARLIE
Filling it, learning, growing,
searching.

ROBERT
Leaving, looking for heart.

JANE
Found some. Lost some.

MELANIE
Lost heart. Lost self.

BERNARD
Back at the start.

JAMES
Looking for HOME.

JANE
It's where the heart is.

SANDRA
Heart.

ALL
It's where the home is.

MELANIE
Everybody will be telling us what to do!!
Our children will want to become our
parents, giving orders and commands!!

Don't take it! Let 'em have it! Don't
let 'em have it! Stand your ground.
There's a lot to lose. Freedom. Pride.
Checkbook. Keys. Home. Self. Life. Hold
on to what you got...till you don't.

CHARLIE

Failures...that's what we call efforts that
didn't make it, dreams that didn't find a
life, ideals left to wander, directions
that went astray, relationships that
dried up, respect that was punctured with
holes. And yet we made it here to a
place that's right, to the place that was
waiting for us to arrive. Failures? We
had some, but had we not...we would not be
here now, and we are, and hopefully happy
to be here. So who has failed?

ROBERT

Last night like many other nights of
late, in deep dark sleeplessness, replays
of days and years toss and tumble me
inside with frowns mostly. Some smiles.
Regrets and successes, a few, mostly
gone. And now, up ahead, seeing those who
are there already. There. Almost gone in
those places where they don't want to
be. What's going on? The lives they live
now. Their eyes tell so much. And make
me wonder... can I do that? Be there. Go
there?

JAMES

Hey, hold on. It's getting way too sad on this porch for me. We need to lighten it up a bit. How 'bout a song? Sing along with me, everybody. You know this one.

ALL
(Standing and singing along to the tune of Don't Cry for Me,Argentina.)

Don't care for me dearest Tina,
I know that I can do it.
I may be old now, but I'm not dead yet,
I still have breath left, don't take it from me.

Don't wait on me dearest Tina,
the truth is, I am still able,
to set the table,
boil, cut, peel, cook and sewsooooooooooooooooo
Don't cry for me dearest Tina
I know you 'aughter,
cause you're my daughter,
but it's too soon now,
I'm just not ready,
can't do this to you……….

(They laugh and giggle with their song!
ALL meander to their rockers and sit,
except BERNARD)

BERNARD
(Remains standing)
Well, that's nice to keep our spirits up,
but how do we keep going, not give up!
Find the Spark! Hope. Strength. Courage.
Desire. We have known hard times. Young
ones don't know. Don't want to hear it.
Oh what marvels we could share. Oh what
input to help avoid pot holes, walls,
ditches, fires, losses. Grief. Lots of
grief. How do we do it in spite of it
all? That's just us. That's who we are!

CHARLIE
(Joins BERNARD)
That's who we are??? Sounds like a
cliché to me. Clichés. We hear lots of
clichés. It's never too late. Get a new
lease on life. Everything's gonna be
alright. You're only as young as you
feel. Get up, get going. Don't worry
about it. Help is just around the corner.
Blue skies are up ahead. It's not the
years in your life but the life in your
years. Live every day like it's your
last. It ain't over till it's over.
Helpful? Not a bit. Sometimes it IS over
before it's over. Some parts. And words
just won't save us.

JANE
(Stands and joins)
About that doctor thing you were talking
about earlier. We all have a few, a
few too many! Some seem to care more

than others. To pay the bill they run us through, like Lucy's candies on the factory tread mill…but to be fair, some take the time to hear us out, about the pain and misery that won't stay away. Some are even helpful with the meds and advice…like when my breath got shorter and my legs moved slow, my doctor said, you need to lighten your load. So I cleaned out my purse!!

JAMES

Let's say tomorrow is the last day, for everybody. What would you do today? What would you want today to be? For me… a soft rain falling quietly from slightly cooled grey skies. Scotch on the side table. Light classical piano on our retro stereo. Candles lighting us both in cozies lying in bed, waiting, holding, remembering. Thankful.

SANDRA

Closets. Attics. Basements. Storage. All that stuff gathered. Go through it. Clean it out. Like the clutter in life. Who's interested? Who cares? Not the kids. Why put them through it? There are some things that are hard to trash. Ok with some replacement, we don't mind a few new things. But don't throw out the old. It is us.

(All but Robert go to their chairs and begin rocking. He hangs back for)

ROBERT

Yeah, you're right, it is us...we are old or we are going to be...but along the way... we found and we lost. We lost and we found... People, Places, Things, Feelings, Ideas, Beliefs, Hopes, Dreams, Realities. We all had those starts and stops along the way, living life on the road most travel. And we are still traveling.

(He sits, passing Jane who jumps up for the last hurray!)

JANE

Don't you just love the way a new day feels? Those few moments when yesterday's memories are slept into a docile file for later. When rest has given birth to new eyes that see a life with energy and hope and a chance to try again!

(Jane takes her seat with all the rockers...EACH delivers a line.)

MELANIE
Inside and outside chances!

BERNARD
Feels good to sit

SANDRA
To rock, to hum, to go numb

CHARLIE
To forget

ROBERT
To wallow

JANE
Use careful balance, action with comfort

JAMES
Rock, but don't rock away.

ALL
(Join in singing The Seniors Song, to the
tune of Let Me Call You Sweetheart)

YOU CAN CALL US SENIORS
SINCE THAT'S WHO WE ARE

STARTS AND STOPS ALONG THE WAY
STILL ALIVE SO FAR

TAKING EACH DAY AS IT COMES
LIVING LIFE SO WELL

SO, YOU CAN CALL US OLD FOLKS
(SENIORS)
BUT WE STILL HAVE MUCH TO TELL.

(LIGHTS FADE OUT DURING FADE OUT, SOMEONE
CHANGES SHOW CARD TO SHOW
"That's It Folks! Thank you.")
(LIGHTS UP FOR CURTAIN CALL)

END

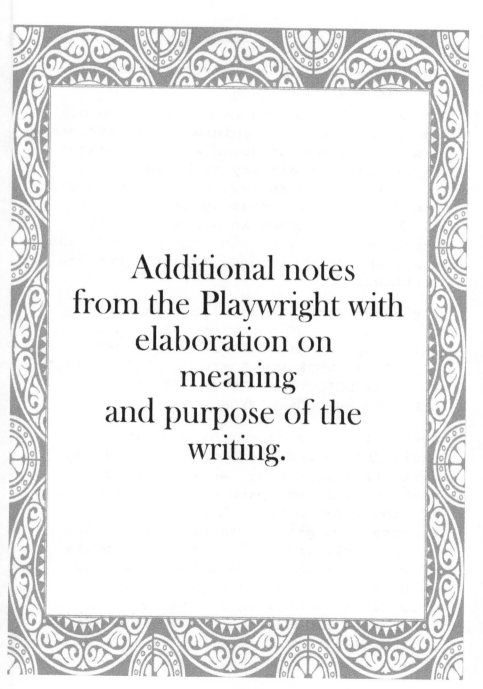

Additional notes
from the Playwright with
elaboration on
meaning
and purpose of the
writing.

Author's In Depth Notes About The Play

This is a story about discovery and acceptance.

GERIATRIC MONOLOGUES is a collection of thoughts, emotions, opinions, revelations and confessions of women and men thought to be old on their way to being older. The notes to themselves about growing old are shared by our messengers with others on the same journey in hopes that the starts and stops on the trip will be less bumpy and hold out more hope for the final destination.

Borrowing freely from Elisabeth Kubler-Rosss' stages of normal grief this is what these monologues are about. THE MONOLOGUES WERE NOT BASED ON THESE STAGES BUT WERE DISCOVERED AFTER THE FACT TO OFFER UP THE CONNECTIONS.

Mourning occurs in response to an individual's realization that one's own death is approaching. As we mourn the death of self we spend different lengths of time working through phases and express each phase more or less calmly or intensely and with different amounts of each. The phases do not necessarily occur in order. We often move between them before achieving a more peaceful acceptance of death which is where the characters in this play finally arrive.

"Remember, grieving is a personal process that has no time limit, nor one "right" way to do it." Kubler-Ross

The oncoming death of you might inspire you to evaluate your own deepest feelings of mortality. As that happens a common thread of hope emerges: As long as there is life, there is hope; As long as there is hope, there is life.

The order of the starts and stops, the phases, is not the same for all and that's ok. The key to understanding them is not to feel like you must go through every one of them. Instead, it's more helpful to look at them as guides in the grieving process — it helps you understand and put into context where you might be.

1. SO THIS IS IT?... when we start becoming aware that we are getting old...we move strongly into denial and often isolation, the first reaction to discovery...realizing that we are not going to live forever... we start to see the reality of the situation. It can be overwhelming, we go in and out of denial, our defenses shift into high gear, we block and hide from the facts...all temporary emotions that carry us through the first wave of pain.

2. SEEMS LIKE YESTERDAY... remembering the younger days of plans and expectations, disappointments and even anger...when we

look back at who we thought we were going to be. We are not ready to admit the reality of now. We feel emotions at our vulnerable core which can be directed and expressed as anger. The anger may be aimed at inanimate objects, complete strangers, friends or family but mostly at our "self" and we are often totally unaware.

3. SIT DOWN AND STAY AWHILE... reflecting on some of the best times. Bargaining can start ...."if only's".... embracing them, holding on to them tightly thinking that's all we have left...memories...while reflecting on the choices that we made... and hidden in our memories are our reactions to feelings of helplessness and vulnerability and a need to regain control-to make things different.

4. WHOSE LIFE WAS IT, ANYWAY!... reflecting on some of the less than good times. The battle begins between depression, feeling sorry for ourselves, and the return of anger...over what was not accomplished and the regret that fills our waking hours, and too often, our sleeping ones, too. Depression is associated with mourning. It is a reaction to practical implications relating to the loss of self. Sadness and regret predominate this type of depression. We worry that, in our grief, we have spent less time with others who depend on us. This phase may

be eased by self-awareness and realizing the need to change. Simple clarification and reassurance may be very helpful and healing. We may need a bit of helpful cooperation and a few kind words. Sometimes all we really need is a hug.

5. OK, NOW WHAT!...doing inventory on what we are thinking and what we're going to do with what we have. Acceptance. Accepting doesn't mean welcoming. We just get to a place of ok...so it's going to be over soon...what do I do about it now and how do I do the last parts in the best possible ways...not only getting through the anger, disappointment, and regrets, but also looking at the possibilities that remain.

6. MY TIME HAS PASSED...embracing that we are where we are- and now, how we are going to live with it. This phase takes us further into the acceptance of the inevitable, and all that goes with the process of ending. Not everybody reaches this stage well if at all. Death comes sooner to some and unexpected or we may never get beyond our anger or denial. Being the strong silent "I can deal with it" type is not necessarily a mark of bravery. To resist the inevitable, to deny ourselves the opportunity to make our peace, can leave us and those around us with even more sadness. This phase is often marked by withdrawal and

uneasy calm. It is not a period of much happiness but must be distinguished from depression.

7. THE ROAD MOST TRAVEL....knowing that the road is going to end, and how we choose to travel the last miles. We begin that last walk, and to some we may appear to go through a final period of withdrawal. It could instead be introspection, evaluating a life lived, and how it was, and what it is. While we may be aware and accepting of our impending demise, which may come from some physical decline our behavior finally says it is natural to reach a place at which social interaction is limited. The dignity and grace shown by the way we approach our dying may well be our last gift to those we leave behind.

Coping with our loss is ultimately a deeply personal and singular experience — nobody can help us go through it more easily or understand all the emotions that we are going through. But others can be involved, friendships and family relationships can deepen, and even fun and humor can find a place as comfort throughout what may be a long process. The best thing we can do is to allow ourselves to feel the grief as it comes over us. Resisting it will only prolong the natural ending and make its arrival all the more unwelcomed.

Geriatric Monologues

Some Smiles and Frowns From the Road Most Travel

The One Act Format of
A Reading Theater Play
with stage directions and production notes
Intended to be taken from the original Two Act
presentation and freely adapted

Written by
Jim R. Rogers

GERIATRIC MONOLOGUES

The One Act Format

Originally produced in February, 2017 by

still learning, inc.

Surfside Beach, SC

Presented by

OLLI, Osher Life Long Learning Institute

Fund Raiser, Myrtle Beach Campus,

Coastal Carolina University, Conway, SC

Premiere of first commercially produced

Presentation, May, 2019, at

Threshold Repertory Theater, Charleston, SC for

PICCOLO SPOLETO 2019

Produced by Dr. Sally Z. Hare

Written and Directed by

Jim R. Rogers and The Cast

GERIATRIC MONOLOGUES

A Reading Theater Presentation of
A One Act Play

By Jim R. Rogers

Based on His Books of poetry *Starts and
Stops Along the Way* and *Looking Around
and adapted* from the original Two Act
play in this play book

CHARACTERS/MESSENGERS
(all in senior years)

BERNARD FIND

Sentimental and melancholy about his life and where he finds himself in it, but resigned. Here we are he says, and here we will be until we're not. Get used to it.

MELANIE MEMORY

In spite of all she sees around her, the growing old of everything, she clings to her past and all that she remembers being the good ole days and longs for them.

CHARLIE CONTENT

He does remember the good stuff, smiles about it, puts his arms around it and lives with all he has to, and complains only a little mostly about what's lost but grateful for what he's found.

ROBERT RANT

Wonders where it all
went and who took it
from him! Can't settle
for what is, what will
be and instead talks
about all that's wrong
and how it could have
been different if he
had been in charge.

JANE DOMORE

Miss Do-gooder
who wants to do more.
The professional
volunteer and
cheerleader nudging all
her aging allies to get
up and get going. So
what! We can't change
it! Stay busy, fill the
mind, move the butt.

JAMES LAMENT

He wants to change it
all. None of it suits
him and he knows in his
heart that maybe he got
it all wrong and he
can't go back. He can
only move forward, if
he chooses, and he's
working on it.

SANDRA FINI

>Digs deeper for
thoughts and beliefs
to comfort her. Of
course it's going to
end, but how and when
and why are there
questions and no one,
even though they
tried with loving
care, has given her
any answers. Are
there any?

SETTING AND TIME

SETTING

The final porch of life where
self-made philosophers act as
messengers and rock to the rhythm and
the beats that formed their lives
and led them to a place of sharing
and remembering, composing acapella
poetic operettas of what's to come
for most.

Lighting and minimal stage props
are involved. Singles with pools of
light or follow spots could be used,
with multiple pools for highlighting
several at a time. The Parts (seven
scenes) of the play are transitioned

with lights fading to black and back
up again with a designated actor
changing the Parts Show Cards as
described in the original two-act
play.

Options and flexibility in staging and
blocking are key to production.

There are seven very different
rocking chairs on stage.

TIME

The last years.

Part 1

So This Is It?

When we start
becoming aware
that we are
getting old.

PART 1

SO THIS IS IT

(The Rocking Porch. Seven empty rockers
of diverse design and size are on an
empty stage. They are arranged in a
conversational setting like on a porch.
BERNARD FINE walks in briskly and
addresses the audience while walking to
what will be HIS rocker. He picks up a
card and reads, then puts it down.

> BERNARD
> Who wants to be old?
> (CHARLIE and MELANIE enter),
> Not he! Not she! Not I!
> (SANDRA, JANE, JAMES enter and meander
> toward rockers)

> SANDRA
> Not we!

> JANE
> But we are.

> JAMES
> So we are.

> ALL
> Yes, we are.

ROBERT
(Entering in haste and irritated)

Leave me be! (He sits hard and talks
soft) But don't leave me alone.

BERNARD
And here we are, on the way to being old.

JAMES
Released from corporate structure,
mandates, orders, expectations.

MELANIE
Raising children.

ROBERT
Raising cain.

JANE
And all that required stuff of the early
years. What will it mean?

SANDRA
We don't know. We've never been here
before. Others have but that's them. Now
it's us.

CHARLIE
Set free to be younger, healthier, empty
nestier, for now.

BERNARD
Decisions still. But new. Like rearranging
the deck chairs on the Titanic.

MELANIE

Where to go. Downsize. Upsize. Gated.
Apartment. Condo. Parent house out back.

ROBERT

Or attached!

JAMES

Retirement community. The village. The
dreaded facility with nurses.

SANDRA

Real old folk yearn to stay.

ROBERT

Home values down. Once a second floor...
status. Now a pain in the rear.

BERNARD

Smart senior friendly home.

JANE

Comfort is what we want. Something more
than shelter.

MELANIE

Where we can be us. Where we have
Memories.

CHARLIE

Where we can age in place. Where we can
be old folks AT home.

(All slowly move to their respective

rockers and either sit or stand beside
them. They are suddenly jerked into
attention by BERNARD)

BERNARD

Zip! Swoosh! Zing! Those are the sounds
it made as it went by. It started
slow enough, young eyes sparkling with
discovery, finding the joy in it, wanting
each day to last longer than the one
before, especially summer. And they did
drag sometimes, mostly when you wanted to
date, to drive, to smoke, to drink, to be
left alone. And then you are. How fast it
goes now. Twice the speed of light. Hard
not to fall off. Not what you thought. Not
what you dreamed. Not where you wanted to
be now. But here you are. So? Cares get
more refined. Time is told in different
ticks and tocks. No stones left to un-turn.
Shirts and pants don't match and once I
wore two different shoes. No one noticed.

(They are all quiet with some smiles and
head shaking in knowing agreement of the
reality)

JAMES

You're not acting like yourself, they
said. I've never been who I am before,
so I don't know if I am myself or not.
The problem is that you don't know what
you want to be when you grow up until you
grow up and then it's most likely too
late to start.

ROBERT

AARP is our badge...to inform, advocate
guide our paths away from ignorance with
dignity, respect...like 91% of us over 65
have at least one chronic condition.

JAMES
(Interjecting)
Thanks for that, AARP!

ROBERT

And sell us really tacky mail order
clothes...shoes that don't need lacing.
Sex aids! Because it's never too late!
And sticks with springs and claws for
reaching where our bodies won't go.

JANE

Calendar pages. One by one they come and
go. They don't mean anything at all unless
we want them to...in the mind, in the heart,
in the desire, in the joy of being alive to
turn another page.

MELANIE

Not much thought at the time about who
our children would be. Not much effort to
help them get there. Here. Maybe too late
to do much now.

JANE
Maybe not.

MELANIE
Maybe not.

JAMES

When we watched the playback of the
Christmas video it hit me over the head
like a ton of bricks. That was me! I was
the old man. While I wasn't looking I had
aged. I had not been unhappy really and
I had been healthy and I had been doing
my work well and supported and loved, so
how the hell did I get so old so fast.
I knew it was time for me to actually
do something with my life, fulfill my
purpose, make a real difference, do
something for god's sake or one morning I
would wake up dead with the excuse that
I had been too busy or I really didn't
know what to do or how to do it...so I did
something else.

SANDRA

(Getting out of rocker and
addressing the group)

How about reunions? Went to one...knew none
until faces came through...wrinkles, spots,
sag, time...and there they were classmates
again shining, smiling, faking,
appearing... in spite of it.

CHARLIE

Stuff! From years. Stacks and layers from
room to room and paths, and detours to
bed. What to do? Where to go? Who wants
what's there...on the walls in the halls,
shelves so full. Boxes now. What to do.
Out they go. Here I stay.

BERNARD

Which way. I could have done this or I
could have done that but not both. How
the hell do we choose?

ROBERT

We don't! It chooses us.

JAMES

Pick and choose. We do have to do some
choosing now. That's what aging offers.
Can't do it all any more, don't even
try, only so many hours, so many weeks,
so many days and nights to go. So many
choices get slimmed down to the few that
we want to do, be with the ones we want
to be with, hug only those who know we
mean it, cut the do list down to done.
I've never done that before. I'm giving
up that never-ending one. Routines
go out, take risks for once, be late
sometimes but be sorry, too, since we
still respect and want to get it back.
They think it's merely idle hours we
do, just staring into space when we're
really just staring into past, looking
to tomorrows, to what's still there. So
let's spend the time that's left the way
we want to spend it. Don't be rude or
sharp of tongue, stay polite and caring,
but be bold and not ashamed to let the
ones who count, count. Just make sure
they know it.

BERNARD

Talking along...and Bam! Can't think of the next word. Stalled in mid-sentence while they wait to see if I make it!

ALL

(Yeah, right, happens to me etc.)

MELANIE

Morning. First check obits. Who's there? Who's not? Not me! Made it another day! So many have so much... long details. Everything they ever did... Awards, Honors, Successes, No failures (Just this one If you can call it that.) Wondering... now mine won't be that much... very little really. Less is more? Life is not measured by the length of the Obit. Is it?

ROBERT

Here's a tribute to Jack Nicholson, 5 Easy Pieces.
She's everywhere. In the drug store. At Hardees and BoJangles. In the grocery deli. At the doc's office. She takes my movie ticket. At breakfast there are many. The hospital has a few. Airplanes too. Big box checkouts for sure. It seems to be just old folks. Males and females both. There must be a school she goes to, to learn just how it goes. She means well, that's for sure, but I always want to say...unless you want to bed me, don't call me honey!

ALL
(ha, ha, and jest and agree,
and then settle
down to a silence...)

TRANSITION....

Part 2

Seems Like Yesterday

Remembering the
younger days of
plans and
expectations.

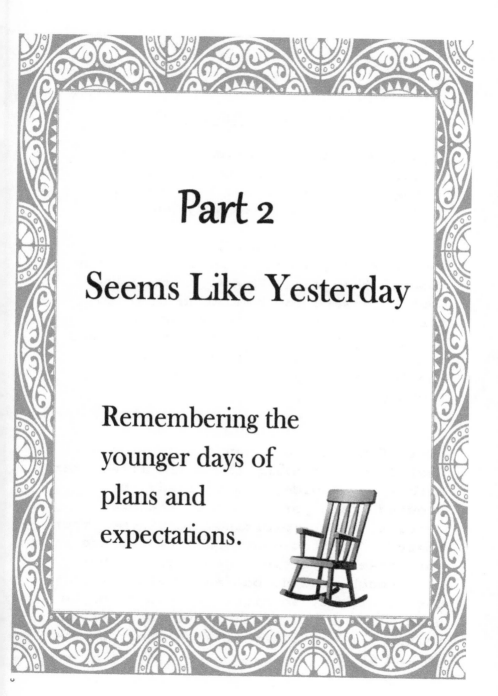

PART 2

SEEMS LIKE YESTERDAY

(MELANIE reaches beside her chair and
pulls out card stands shows card and
reads "Part two Seems Like Yesterday"
puts the card away and)

MELANIE
Remember long distance phone calls? How
special they were. How we planned them.
Looked forward to them. Used them only
for very special occasions. Amazing
miracle of the times. How I miss those...
and hand-written notes of thanks...of
"hello how are you? I've been thinking
about you lately."

CHARLIE
Out of the house I went... away from all
that I knew, feeling the world like never
before... eyes wide... heart ready... brain
growing... each person I met, the one I
thought, fresh, exciting, worrisome, then
scary. Then too many... one, two, three
more teachers giving, getting some but
not enough. One so odd and would not fit.
One so bright, so right, so wrong. Maybe
home was best. I should have just stayed
in one place. No way it's so... just go and
go and GROW.

JAMES

It was supposed to be simple, clear,
direct, and even easy. But it just got
complicated. There was no way a young
and idealistic boy from a Norman Rockwell
town could have prepared for what he got...
On-the-Job training.

ROBERT

Whatever I have is what I've got. No
more. No less. It's mine. I worked hard,
lived long, loved many, lost some,
laughed a lot. And cried. Whatever I have
it's mine. Whatever it is.

MELANIE

Like Family? Family. The glue that holds
us together. Gets too hot and melts. And
the pieces fall apart, but stay sticky.

SANDRA

When do you know it's time for a change?
Where does the idea first come from?
A distant spot of sail on the mind's
horizon, gliding slowly toward you
getting fuller and bigger and closer and
stronger as it sensitizes your knowing of
the wind.

JANE

Does it grow like a seed in the ground,
getting larger and healthier as its
environment of need waters and nurtures
it to blossom and beautifully lulls you
into the notion that you had better move
from where you are. Sometime soon.

ROBERT

Or maybe it starts as a mental cold sore,
causing just a hint of the pain that is
to come unless you do something but of
course you don't know all that unless
you've gone through such change before
and if you have, then why are you letting
yourself in for all that shit again?

MELANIE

It could be that you are just sick and
tired of being sick and tired as the
12-steppers say. You could be just stuck
in a mud rut, adjusted to the goo and
slow movement and not do anything but
stay stuck. Then, there's that classic
cliché when the pain of staying is worse
than the pain of leaving. That's when you
have to change. To do otherwise would be
totally foolish.

BERNARD

And yet being foolish doesn't seem to
matter. When I am deep into dysfunctional
comfort, I don't care if I'm foolish or
not; I care about whether or not I am
happy. But, even then happiness is so
fleeting. One minute high, another low.
I always feel empty when I'm happy…and
guilty. It won't last long and there are
so many others who aren't. So, I don't
do anything.

JAMES

They say that's a decision. It is just too much trouble. I don't think I can change. Not if my life depends on it. Maybe it does. Naa. What's the big deal? I'm just hot, that's all and I need to cool this room down. Now let's see. Is it up to cool or down to cool? Never can get that straight. Should I take a chance, or wait for somebody who knows? I think I'll wait. For now. Maybe.

CHARLIE

Decades. So many. So many of us. So many paths we took. So many stories to tell. So much happened in our decades. So many of us. So alike. So different.

ROBERT

So what!

BERNARD

Passion. Used to drive me. Got me up. To go. To do. (ROBERT interjects with a huh?) Got me up for that, too. Knew I could energize when needed. Get it done. Make 'em applaud. See how good I am. Where has it gone? Away from me, and I can't seem to find it again, and I had nothing to say about it.

JANE

Oldies but goodies. We listened to music
that we love, danced closely, whispered
stuff that came to be. Doing it still.
Loving it still. Now that we are REAL
Oldies, REAL Goodies.

JAMES

Some days it's hard to just put one foot
in front of another. Afternoon and early
evening nods come and I can't stop them.
Tired. Run down. Bored. Indolent. Snorts
wake me. Ashamed when I don't respond
to a question, react to a birdie, or
participate in conversation. Is this the
sleep before the BIG sleep? Tryouts!!!

SANDRA

Little things you never thought to be
hard, are. Just getting out of a chair
without soreness, pain, grunting,
pushing, pulling, regretting, limitations
that seem to come with the territory.
Eventually, accepting.

BERNARD

Sitting in a room, crowded with interested
guests hanging onto the speaker's words
of wisdom. Except me. Hard to hear from
where I am- 6th row. Ashamed to cup my
hand over my ear. Both sure signs of age.

ROBERT
(Pleased with his add-on)
And vanity!!

Vanity? I still have that, and how about
dreams? Dreams? Boy, did I have a few.
Wanted to be a cowboy and ride horses and
shoot guns and kill bad guys and be the
hero of my life. I had to let go of that.
Wanted to be the quarterback, and make
touchdowns, and win exciting games, get
the girls and be a champion all-star. I
had to let go of that.
Wanted to be a great lover, with lots of
conquests, play the field for all it was
worth before finding the most beautiful
wife to be mine forever.
I had to let go of that.
Wanted to be a Hollywood star, admired by
the world, with a fan club and magazine
covers and the most cheered acceptance
speech for Oscar.
I had to let go of that

Wanted that perfect family, with that
perfect wife, perfect gender children,
beautiful home in the best neighborhood,
driving the most expensive car on the
block.
I had to let go of that.
Wanted a vacation home, on the lake in
the mountains, with an inboard motor
boat and a dock with water sports,
excellent restaurants near-by and envious
neighbors. I had to let go of that.
Instead I got to be a respected
accountant, an effective lineman, a shy
woman magnet, the president of Kiwanis,

owner of a mortgage-free home in the nice
suburbs; after one divorce, a perfect
wife with intelligence and beauty, and
four unequaled children, two of each,
all college graduates, and was voted
volunteer of the year when I was 70. I
hold on tight to all that.

                    All
          (Give him a little applause and
                 atta boy's.)

                   JANE
This I know for sure...sitting too long
in one place feeling like the world has
passed you by and woe is you because
you're old will push you deeper into the
pluff mud of nothing into more nothing
until you disappear! But doing something,
any something, will move you...activate
yourself, and one grows into more, then,
many and many gets you going again.
What's that those shoe people say...Nike...

                  ROBERT
                Just do it!!

                   JANE
Yeah, that's it...Just do it! They got it
right, alright.

                  BERNARD
Use to be just three channels and
sometimes less...early morning, day time,
until midnight...cheap entertainment on the

tube. Now, Wow!! A vastland of choices,
twenty-four hours, seven days, three
hundred sixty five. Everywhere you look,
listen. So much there!

ROBERT
(Another zinger for him)

Not much there!!

Yeah, and what about all those medicines
for whatever ails us? All through the
vastland, countless commercials telling
us who to be, how to be, when to be, what
to be…And the medications…The best of
all! Helping anew…but watch out for "The
Sides"… nausea, headaches, bloat, weight
loss,

All
(Others get it and join In with their
own contributions to the list…randomly
shouting out.)

SANDRA
or gain…hives…

JAMES
HBP…LBP…gout…

BERNARD
depression…anxiety…mood swings…

CHARLIE
lost wages...shortness of breath...
shortness...tallness...mother in law blues...

MELANIE
mass murder tendencies...Rose hater...
Terrorism Tactics...even death...

(Now, everybody jumps in with their own
creations of maladies to cure until it is
chaos of over-talk)

(ROBERT picks it back up and closes it
out as they all get a hoot and a holler
with their contributions and the
silliness of the pharmaceutical world
on TV)

ROBERT
Yeah, ok, whoa...And so on...and on and on.
Unbelievable!!! Not me! I'm sticking with
what I've got.

(With comments like "me too", "that's
what I think"...they all slowly move back
toward their rockers and settle back in)

BERNARD
Aging they say is all in your head...
that's true except the parts that are
in your knees, your hips, your joints
and assorted other parts where aches and
pains hang out and greet you daily, just
to remind you and keep your head from
getting too lonely.

JANE

Along the way...many starts, many stops,
checking in to see what was there for me.
Found and lost. Lost and found... People,
Places, Things, Feelings, Ideas, Beliefs,
Hopes, Dreams, Realities, Starts and
stops along the way.

TRANSITION

Part 3

Sit Down And

Stay Awhile

Reflecting on some
of the best times
relived and
remembered.

PART 3
SIT DOWN AND STAY A WHILE

(CHARLIE picks card beside chair
and reads to audience, puts it down
then takes out letter and pulls chair a
bit closer to the audience.)

CHARLIE

I'd like to share a note I wrote to my
late wife. My life wife. We had been
married almost four years at the time:
"Love has not been a stranger to me...I
have known her. She embraced my mother
and me and my father in an entirely
different way. She showed me her way with
my brothers and cousins and aunts and
grandmother and friends, although looking
back that may have been something else.

"As I grew, she showed me more and let me
love a wife in a way that I could then.
There was care and caring but there was
always still me. Later, she introduced me
to passion and that was good. And then
came romance and then came otherness. Out
of nowhere love matched me to another
who knew her in a different way, but a
way that made me feel Loved. I finally
arrived at the ultimate love, I thought.
She gave two a connection and a bond, and
that, too, was good. And then she changed
course. Love was redefined.

It became something else. Romance waned.
Passion cooled. Only care remained.
And otherness. Still. Confused and
despondent. How could it have CHANGED TO
something else?

"And now I know. It changed to become.
Love has gently warmed her way deep
into a place I didn't know existed. She
has revealed a part of her that goes
way beyond anything imagined. She has
let me have this time with her very own
incarnation. She has given me herself.
She has given me you."

I found this note as I was going through
her letter box last month. She kept it
for 47 years. I hope she took it out and
read it every now and then, to make up
for those years that I neglected to tell
her how much I loved her. I hope she did
that.

SANDRA
(Remembering)
So sweet, Charlie, thank you. Makes
me remember Spooning. The greatest
pleasures and comforts of the day, any
day are those when the last light is out
the dogs are quiet, the nite lights are
soft and I snuggle up and hold you gently
firm being just where I want to be... then
it's your turn to hold me. Even better.
What a fit!

JANE

Finding joy was a daily discovery in youth... except for the disappointments that came...the hurt...the heartbreaks. Made me strong and wise so today I can still have joy...with the disappointments, the hurt, the heartbreaks.

MELANIE
(Taking her time and lightening up to BERNARD)

Will you remind me to tell them to fix the overhead light in the car?

BERNARD
Who's going to remind me?

MELANIE
Let's leave notes. Remember to do that.

BERNARD
You remember to do that. And remember to remind me to remind you.

MELANIE
Ok. Ok, I forgot. You remembered.

BERNARD
You forgot. I remembered.

MELANIE
We two do make a good <u>one</u>.

CHARLIE

Many times, I'd say, closer please.
She'd say, I can't get any closer. I'd
say try. She did. And did.

BERNARD

Difficult getting through the days feeling
like no purpose. Tired of doing stuff I
don't really want to do. Tired of going
just to be going. Tired. Just tired.
Then she comes in, I smile and want her,
filled with energy, forgetting tired. That
stuff comes from another place.

SANDRA

Grandchildren come and go...like children
leaving us behind. Their life. Their
choice. Like we did. But before taking
off, what pride, what angst, what pain,
what worry, what joy. What memories.

ROBERT/JANE
(Alternating lines)

You'll tell me if I have food in my
beard? If you'll tell me I have spinach
on my tooth. If I talk too loud. If I
talk too much. If I repeat myself. If my
jokes aren't funny. If the blackheads
show. If the hairs need tweezers. If
I eat too fast. If I'm unkind. If I'm
fading fast. If I'm still pretty. If I'm
still a hunk? Oh, yes. Still. OK then.
We're fine.

MELANIE

We did some things. A place where smiles
come easy. The couch is a teddy bear for
many. Finding comfort even in discord.
The place is safe enough for honest
words. The time together renews the bond.
The people there embrace you. There was a
hole, now pushed way back, filled in with
growth that time can give. Gifts and food
and care abound. That place we nurture
and get it from. How they long to greet
the roots. We made it strong and it
holds us well. Home.

SANDRA
(Slow and sadly)

One, two, three, four, five, six…The
monthly visits now. Agreed places where
we go together…Hand in hand…But not in
step. We were never really in step, thank
god, but we were really in love.

CHARLIE

Movies have always been favorites.
Saturday afternoon horse operas,
cartoons, shorts, classic features and
most not. Right through the many years
to computer generations of Avatars and
Transformers and walking dead zombies.
So many movies warped my sense of time.
Pieces of lives lived in scenes sewed
together with music, effects, explosions
created unreal time lines, hiding the
worst… the days between are the hardest
to take.

BERNARD

You. You are the you in YOUrself. Who Else could be there? You are the one to think, to see, to do, to be. Who else knows you as you know you? Only you.

TRANSITION

Part 4

Whose Life Was It, Anyway!

Taking stock of some
of the disappointments
and dislikes that
accompany us
on the trip.

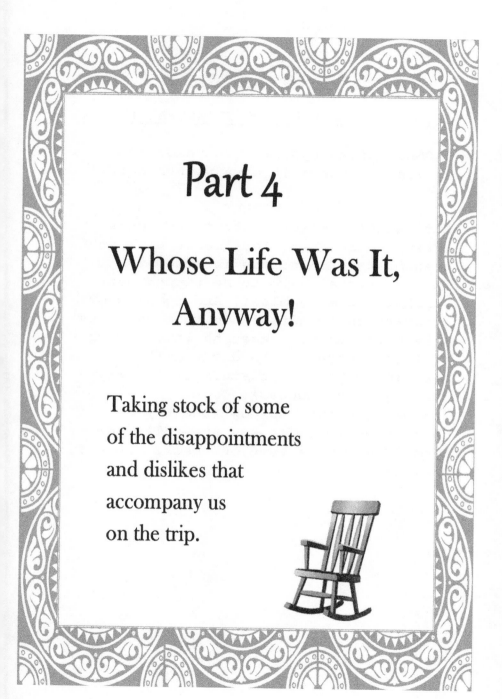

PART FOUR

WHOSE LIFE WAS IT ANYWAY!!

(ROBERT picks up card and reads it to audience, throws it down with a huff!!)

ROBERT

Irritations on small stuff come more often and quicker. Impatience with an open drawer. Those ads inserted in magazines that have to be ripped out. Stickers on my apples!! And remains of stickers on my gifts! How thin can they make paper anyway? Wasting time trying to turn a page.   The dirty dish in the sink.   Stacks of stuff in the way
(Moving into sadness)
The way she says no now… the way she never says yes. The way she rolls her eyes. The way we turn our backs, in bed. In life.

BERNARD

So many times, I feel like screaming!
Unfair Unjust Rude Ignorant Incompetent
Intolerant Inconsiderate Mean. Hands
tied. Mouth shut. Inside heat... with
nowhere to go.

JAMES

I knew this guy. He often envied those
who knew why they had been born. The
natural athlete, or explorers or teachers
who never even thought about being
anything else. They came to do a certain
job, and they did it, got very good at it
and were honored for having given their
all to a job or to others. He could have
gone in so many different directions.
He had some talent in many areas...and
choosing one or even two proved to be
melancholy now in his last years. He
often wondered if he had gone in another
direction, what would his life had been
like. If he had chosen to pursue his
first love, or even his second, would it
have made any difference in how he felt
now? I wonder how his wife might have
felt about his having those questions.

CHARLIE

I've had thoughts about it all. Maybe tell
her how lucky he may have been, now that
he has been dead for a year. Cancer got
him young. Been thinking about it all and
how dying early takes care of any old age
second guessing...and wondering about what

comes next...and whether we did all we wanted
to or... we bog down in the misery of lost
life and regrets. She should know this.

MELANIE

No. Don't Tell Her. She knows.

ROBERT
(Happily changing the mood)
Hey, there were these two senior seniors
giving each other the middle finger in the
parking lot at the post office. Drew quite
a crowd. Both right. Both wrong. Does it
really matter? Seemed to, to them.

BERNARD

And then...we get to the real stuff, the
stuff of life. First with the prostate,
Sitting to pee. Standing took too long
to finish. Multi stops on trips...Movies
not over two hours. Biopsies...Benign...
Lucky...But still got the roto rooter.
Still sitting. Now challenged by all low
commodes with high water!

ROBERT

You know, even the most intimate friends
never know about the sagging balls in
the toilet bowl water. (ALL DO DOUBLE
TAKE SMILE) This is the age when men make
close friends of urinals!

CHARLIE

Getting shorter was a surprise. Another unexpected gift of aging. And...honey-do lists she gave me and I would respond... I'll get to that,

ROBERT

And, I'll get to that, to that, and that...

JAMES

I'll get to that, and I'll get to that, too...

BERNARD

And I'll get to that, and that, and I'll get to that!

(AFTER A BEAT, IN SYNC)

ALL

Pretty soon now!!! (They all laugh at themselves and settle back in.)

JANE

When you get old, your body starts making noise...starts talking to you...snap crackle and pop joints with vocal accompaniment... Groans, moans, ows and ohs and a few dammits. Hurts to move... to roll over ... to readjust. It hurts to change positions... and opinions.

ROBERT

TV is my challenge. So much wrong and I catch them at it! Yelling at the stupidity

of officials, of commercials. Politicians/
City officials. Did I say City officials?
Celebrities. Did I say Politicians? You
think that's good! I think it stinks! No
one cares.   I do.

BERNARD
Expand-a-waist pants! Genius. Fit like
a glove. Pride lost to bulge. Why not
expand-a-shirts? Now go to Goodwill
after 20 years. Button strain... then up a
larger size...on the cheap...breath holding
time reduced 20%!

SANDRA
Senior ballet! One-legged dancing...not
holding on... putting foot in pants, under
ware, panty hose, finding balance, being
graceful... And fearful that it will only
get worse.

MELANIE
Reinventing ourselves is what we're
supposed to do, but I like me as I am.
They laugh at us. I know. I used to. We
wear strange clothes. They're old. Why
get new? They think we have bad taste.
They don't know that we just don't give
a shit. (PAUSE) We don't deserve it
all. Not all. But some for sure... Loud...
Self-centered... Selfish... Demanding... Don't
listen...Talk...A lot... About Our lives...
Where we came from...What we did... Who we
were................ When we were.

JAMES

I used to laugh under my breath at the way some old folks dressed. The leisure suits, the matching nylon sweat suits with the required stripe, or the twin tee shirts with "I'm with stupid" printed on the fronts, the Velcro strap shoes, the awful taste in the matching of clothes, stripes with checks, yellows with greens, greens with blues, (my mother would croak) those dumb Henry Fonda On Golden Pond hats, and the list is endless. I used to think it was because they had no money as well as no taste. They lived on a fixed income and couldn't afford nice new clothes and someone to advise them on what to choose to wear. Now that I am one of them, it's not money.

CHARLIE

It's what JANE just said...we don't care... Some of us, that is. We aren't trying to win another's heart, approval, blessing, promotions, or anything. Why should we care? Nobody sees us anyway. And if we really wanted them to, then wearing this stuff is the surest way to get their attention! What was it they used to tell us as young parents? Children need attention. If they don't get any, they will do something to get it. They would rather have negative attention than no attention at all. It must be true.

ROBERT

The older I get, the more pissed off I get. It's no wonder old people get cranky with age. They see the end... they didn't get it all done... they didn't do anything they wanted to do much less everything they wanted to do. No time to start over. Trying to contribute..... Get disrespect... demeaned...Discouraged. Pissed off! Like never before! I saw this poster recently of a lovely lady and her quote...the older I get, the more people can kiss my ass!

(Pauses, OTHERS RESPOND!! takes a long breath and continues)

I'll tell you what bothers me! People who park in no parking, handicapped, wrong lane, wrong way, take up two parking spaces, biggest suv on the block. People in movies talking loud at wrong times, putting their feet, sometimes bare feet, on the back of the seats in front of them, leaving during the credits, blocking the view of others. Rudeness! Inconsiderate! Hard to tolerate rudeness. It's all about that for me. Pissed off. Again.

BERNARD

Sagging comes slowly but it comes. What was here, moved to there. Changing waist, other parts, too. Not seen but felt. Hell NO to T shirts and all tight fitting anythings. Avoiding mirrors, reflective

windows, any attention at all! Anything
that will show you to yourself!

JANE
Educate me? I don't want to know all
that stuff that will make me happier,
healthier, richer, wiser, skinnier,
smarter, social. I just want to be
Me. The real me. Hair growing where it
shouldn't... not growing where it should.
You know; hair today, gone tomorrow! Skin
gets thin...letting through those dark
places, the red, black, blue road maps
that were hiding there all along.

JAMES
All the money went to someone. Not me.
And now I sit wishing, regretting,
wondering, mad as hell, sad, too, and
not knowing what's next. Plans I had
derailed. Accidents. Fate. Illness.
Injury. Things happen. Unintentional
detours along the way. Plans changed.
There's no turning back. I can rewind and
look at it... pause and reflect on it. But
it's done. Can't change what was. Can
change what might be!

BERNARD
Tired of doing it. (Remark from ROBERT)
Not that. We still do that. Some don't
think it works after 50. Tired of pinching
pennies. Writing monthly checks. Waiting
for a real person on the phone. Waiting
for the kids to call. A thank you note.

Brushing teeth. Combing my hair. Taking
pills. Doctors' appointments. Procedures
Required. Social time. Bridge. Walking at
the mall. Shopping. Golf. Drinking. Too
much. Not remembering what's good.

MELANIE
Yeah, about picking out our clothes.
Comfort not style… Except to impress the
others at the dragged-to socials, human
service meetings, worships, weddings,
funerals… A lot. So few look. Fewer care.

JANE
Can't talk about Hemorrhoids, Gout,
Gas, Pimples, Flatulence, Psoriasis,
Operations, Procedures, Children,
Politics, Religion, Savings, Stock
market, Neighbors, In laws. But We do.

SANDRA
Mom chose Family Dollar Sweats. Gave
her Belk's blouses that stayed in the
boxes… still the sweats. Why Mom? Easier.
Finding, choosing, maintaining, cold
wash, no iron; three colors: black, grey,
and navy blue; soft, Comfy. We were
frustrated, bewildered.   Now
we know. How smart she was. Now it's us…
just nicer sweats. More colors.

MELANIE
Growing apart it's called now. Growing
together it should be. Could be. What
have we become? Where is what we were?

Along the way, the disconnect that we
vowed would not be us. And here we are...
together but apart... wondering, grieving
what was. Hoping for something else...
something that was.
Again.

TRANSITION

Part 5

OK.
Now What?

Doing inventory on
how we are thinking
and what we're
going to do with
what we have.

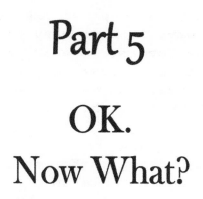

PART 5

OK. NOW WHAT?

(SANDRA picks up card reads puts down
and)
Beliefs. Practicing what we preach. Or
not. So many ways from so many places.
Baskin-Robbins flavors. It works most of
the time. Some think everybody else is
wrong. Same goals... Heaven not hell. Will
we get where? Up to each.

CHARLIE
Time: it's been going on for some time
now and I think I have learned some
things. Here's one. I don't waste as
much time as I used to. The process
of getting to depression and coming
out again is shorter. I can go to the
suicide mode and up to euphoria almost
immediately without messing around with
all that stuff in between.

MELANIE
Brick By Brick I build my wall... Ten
feet wide and twice as tall. Yes, I
wonder when they say "That Wall, is it
protecting you or is it in your way?"

BERNARD
Self Help. Book shelves lined with
volumes... soul searching philosophy...

simple and deeper poetry...for sale psychology from infomercials. A lot has helped a little... a little has helped a lot. A store house of searching, a library of life. Along with others I've needed all the help I could get to face the unexpected events of life. In it all I made a find... the best single aid for grief, loss, depression, frustration, confusion, rejection, desperation, anger, hurt, loneliness and all of the more, is to have a little money in the bank.

SANDRA

Oh, how I wish! I saw this on TV the other day. Something called Anthropology Navigator. Not sure if it's real but it made sense to me. Pilots, sailors and hard-headed husbands use it, too. Dead Reckoning. Explained by them as, to know where you are, you have to know where you've been. What it looked like, felt like, what it sounded like, who you were when, who you wanted to be. Then you know if you've arrived.

JAMES

Well, I'm not so sure I've arrived yet... still working on it. (To Audience) Do you see me? Raise your hand if you see me...good...so many people don't see us old folks, do they?...I guess it takes one to see one.

It's hard not being who I was, but now
it's so. I still am some, at least the
parts that count. Some things don't and
it's a good thing since hair is gone,
muscle is less, get up and go is missing,
joints need oil. Age is sneaky, you know
it's back there lurking, waiting, all
of a sudden, overnight there it is in
the mirror, in others' eyes; it's the
disappear potion and it works as you
are no longer seen. No one takes you
seriously. Old stories are just that
and they don't count for much except to
you. Only a few regrets and only because
of sadness and pain you may have caused
and you have no idea about what's next;
how could you really? How could anybody?
No one has been there to tell it, to
share it, so you live each hour like
the last and mull it over and try not
to hurt again. Or we might end up on
the line somewhere believing that what
has been was a cruel joke or maybe an
extraordinary privilege. Of course. It's
Both.

JANE

Good Morning! I love the way a new
day feels. Those few moments when
yesterday's memories are slept into a
docile file for later. When rest gives
birth to new eyes that see a life with
energy and hope and a chance to try
again.

MELANIE

Staying so long keeps so much stuck in place. Pictures on walls. Nicks and knacks on tables. Shelves crowding. Closets full of never-worn favorites. No room for more. Stuff accumulates over time Easy to see the floors the doors show wear. But a slight movement brings discomfort. Dogs bark. Even the dust feels at home.

CHARLIE

Not too concerned about our appearance. Some anyway. We wear old clothes...worrying about not spending that money we may need for older age, and not to burden the children and spouses. We have nothing to gain by looking great no wo/man's hand to win, no job to compete for, no seeking approval from others 'cause they don't see us anyway and the young folks say look at that old fart with stripes and checks and pants too short and hat not right and no style shirt and hair a mess. And we smile. (Long pause then bursting with) WHO inspires us?!!

ALL

We do!!!!

JAMES

I'm not as good as I thought I was... not as smart, not as special. I don't know what happened. Hard to admit We don't know it all. Mother had drawers too

stuffed to open. Why, mom? Not smart.
Doesn't even make sense.   Now you
should see my drawers. If I could open
them.

SANDRA

My hectic Busy life is slowing down now.
My plan as I have the time to think often,
actually clearly, is to think clearly.
I am learning that there are many more
people than I who are more special than
I or who have probably suffered the same
haunting thoughts as I that they too were
special and had a special contribution to
make in their lives and wonder if it's
too late.

JANE

No news is good news. Better than what
we see, hear day after day after day.
Printed. Television. Radio. Painting
pictures of how bad it is, how bad it's
going to be… and no slowing down! So no
more news for me. I'll make my own, thank
you.

BERNARD

Epiphany on the roof. Due to age I
had to change the way I do things. No
longer strength, athleticism. Balance
now has to be. Planning, not taking
risks, taking breaks, using my brain and
staying focused… like not stepping on the
electrical cord and watching my feet slip
out from under me and rolling me off the

roof's edge, smashing to the ground in one
large grunt with something broken that
will send me to the emergency room and
her into a dither. While I was creating
this new approach to living longer and
taking great pride in my discovery and
losing my focus on the task, I stepped on
the electrical cord. Nope. I did not slip
down. Worse. I allowed myself a couple
of well-phrased ouch words loud enough
for the preacher in his yard next door to
hear, who responded to my "Jesus Christ!"
with "Praise The Lord!" And I heard her
coming. So much for that.

MELANIE
It's building. The complexity of it all
overwhelms me and paralyzes my brain. A
global community and so flat we can see it
all at one time. Too much to take in. It
freezes me in place.

JANE
Old people are problems. We hear that. Of
course we are. One of our entitlements.
Should we be? We can be more the
solution. Nobody thinks to ask. Don't
wait. Tell them! Speak up! Risk it.
What do we have to lose?

SANDRA
Dogs. Einstein and Eleanor Roosevelt. Not
kidding. On the daily walk as long as the
journey is underway, high spirits and
jaunty. But when they sense that we are

about to end it and return home, spirits
fall and meandering delay sets in.   As
soon as we sense the journey beginning to
end we slip into depression and despair
rather than enjoying to the fullest the
time on the trip we have left and one
more sniff of what's there.

ROBERT

Can't do it. Can't stop. Can't try.
Can't go. Get angry. No! Get really
angry! Mad! Pissed off! That might help.
Who?   I know I'm Right! How could this
be wrong? Why can't everybody be like
me? Why can't everybody be just like me?
Mr. Perfect. Then we wouldn't have any
problems.

Do I hear you smiling?

BERNARD

All my life there was this feeling way
down deep inside me that I was special.
All my life I felt that there was
something unique I was supposed to do.
All my life I found myself out of step
pretty much most of the time. All my life
I kept looking and listening for the
guidance, the direction, the way. All my
life I wondered how it would happen, when
it would happen and how I would handle
it. All my life it seemed to be around
the next corner.   Hold on a little while
longer and you'll find it. All my life
the place I thought I was to be wasn't

the place for long enough to be the final place. Here's where I made my mistake I actually believed what I was told... that what I ended up choosing to be, mattered. As we age we find that with rare exceptions, the rank-and-file common man has little to do with what happens in the world. But we do have something to do with what happens in our hearts. That's pretty special to me.

JAMES

There are days I feel like I am waking up after a long sleep. Now that I am slowing down my brain activity and my physical to-do list, there is more time for me to see things I haven't noticed in a long time, or never did, or thought they were too menial to dwell on at the time. I find myself seeing people, places, and things...behaviors for the first time. Things I know... we all have feelings of wanting recognition, approval, applause. Adults and children alike need involvement, engagement, inclusion, interest, care... and if we don't get it we become sad, disappointed, resentful, angry, uncooperative, and we act out in many ways.

ROBERT

Like...ranting!...I've tried that. Done it a lot. It always seems to end with no results but rather regrets over embarrassing those around me and myself. I want so hard to be Atticus Finch, the original one. I want to be emotionally mature, conversationally brilliant, effective in my convictions and persuasion efforts. I think I missed that boat.

BERNARD
Just because I am one, I don't have to be one. An old person. I'm not gonna be one. I refuse to be one. I don't like what I see and I don't want to look like them!

JAMES
Well, good luck with that! This is what happens to us old folks as we realize that we are going to die. Not sooner or later, but sooner than later. We see it beginning to lift its head yonder on the horizon and it scares the hell out of some of us. We're not ready to go yet. We still have some fish to fry. We want to see the grands grow up and prove that generations do improve with each cycle. We want to see if there is something we can do to change it all and make it better. Not only our lives past, but the lives of the future old people who, as young folks now, have no idea what's ahead of them. You know what? Neither do I.

BERNARD
Yeah, all of us can say that. We don't have crystal balls. But this I know for

sure, because we have less and less
say-so, or any power, or any sense of
accomplishment or achievement...we do a
whole lot of criticizing. Gives us
artificial power, a manufactured coping
skill to deal with failure or a sense
of it at least or makes us feel that we
know better. For a while there, as I
unconsciously began to feel the pull of
time gone and not complete, I started to
criticize everything...I mean everything.
Well, not her, even though she did do
some stuff that drove me crazy, but with
her, I bit the bullet. I didn't want to
sound like a cantankerous old curmudgeon.

ROBERT

Yeah... I criticized the hiway construction,
a natural target. I didn't think they
knew what they were doing. Why did they
do this this way instead of that? Just
didn't make sense. The on- and-off ramps
were stupid and the way the DOT patched
the roads was a joke. And the town crews,
forget about it! I even criticized the new
football stadium they were building at our
university. It went up impressively but I
just knew that they hadn't measured right.
The playing field didn't look like it was
100 yards. It couldn't be. I actually
laughed at myself for that. That's when
I knew I was getting better...healthier.
More hopeful I think some people call that
"aging into wisdom." I hope so. I could
use a little wisdom about now.

JANE

Maybe that's what's happening to me. The
first faint colors of my own mortality
have begun to glow around the outer
defenses of my living. Barely visible
now, I know they are there. Breathing
down my neck. Mostly they are shades of
foreboding gray. Not those fifty shades,
either...did you see that movie?

BERNARD
(Interjecting)
"Yeah, twice."

JANE

Smirks and continues, Is that wisdom??
Don't think so! My grey is just one
color...dark...but I have to say...sometimes
and getting more often, it turns into
many pastels, and they are pleasing and
even inviting. And they will get brighter
and closer. And when that happens, I
wonder what I'll do?

SANDRA

Wondering. It was my normal state of
urgency. I have lived most of my life
with a to-do list and I was damned good
at getting stuff done. I was raised
to believe that you are your work and
your achievements are the shining stars
of success in our world. I had a work
ethic so big I almost choked on it. One
of many positives handed down to me by
my Dad. Character. That was his big

thing. He was the most honest man I ever knew. He worked hard his entire adult life, finally living a few years with his camellias and azaleas before cancer got him at 61. I can't cheat. I can't lie. Well, I can't out and out lie. Whites and omissions, yeah, but they don't count in today's world. They counted to my dad, though.

BERNARD

It's interesting what happens to us as we find ourselves with more time. Today, I didn't feel stress and pressures of taking care of the to-do list items, since there are few left on the list these days. So a lot of them fell through the cracks. And next month they will bite me in the ass.

MELANIE

I have time to stop and talk with neighbors without feeling like I have to hurry and get on to whatever is next. I had time to go through the dry cereal inventory, sorting out the old stuff and putting the keepers into attractive plastic containers, and I even tore off the box top so we would know what dwelled therein. Why do we do that? Find ways to spend more time on frivolous tasks.

JANE

Maybe to help us feel a sense of accomplishment, like we really are doing something useful. Something we can actually complete. I know that's why I like to work in the yard, now. I used to hate it, because I was too busy doing other more important stuff. You know what I mean, don'cha?

CHARLIE

Yeah, I know. I used to pour my diet coke kinda like I did parenting...fast and on the run. And the coke always foamed over leaving a mess for me to clean up and then pour some more. Now, I have more time. I do the slow pour. I stand there pouring till the glass is full and no foam or mess to clean up. (Looks to audience and smiles) Smart!

TRANSITION

Part 6

My Time Has Passed

Accepting that we are
where we are and
how we are
dealing with it.

PART 6
MY TIME HAS PASSED

JANE gets the next card, reads it and puts it down...then...

Volunteer. That's what we do and we do it well. They need us. They love... us... or not. They want us to help. We do. Them. Us.

JAMES
Something so mundane... Becoming so important. Today, I polished my shoes. My black ones, then my brown ones, buffed my suede ones, new strings in my New Balance all-purpose. Took my time and did a good job. Didn't feel rushed to get on to something else... polishing my shoes was the something else. It had been such a long time since I had done it myself. Most times had them done at the shoe shop. Stuff done by others. You know, we busy people living life like we're supposed to, fast, quick, always in a hurry, just touching the surface of things, too often forgetting value. Like how important it was to have an unhurried conversation with my teen-age son. (Looks down) Nice shoes? (Looks back up) Lost son.

MELANIE
Still doing the things I like. Going

where I can Now There is more. More time
To do and go and be. More of others. More
of me.

JANE

We matter. Just when I thought I knew it
all, I didn't. Just when I thought I was
tall, I came up short. Just when I was
on top, I fell. Just when I was loved, I
lost. Just when I gave up, I got up. We
matter!

SANDRA

So, here I am. An old person. We all
are. I have heard from lots of sources
that we are now in the elder ranks...a
position in life, I, for one, accept.
Because now, when someone asks me to do
something, I say. Sorry, Elders don't <u>do</u>.
We advise, we consult, we point things
out...point to things like, she doesn't
look 60 to me...more like 80! Or, don't go
anywhere with him, he drives like a mad
man. And he'll hit on you. If you give him
an inch, he'll go for the mile.

So, now, as the elders we are or are
becoming, and as elders in our gained
wisdom, we have all the answers, you
know. We feel it's our obligation to
share those answers with you, some of
them at least. Ones that always worked
best for us...like

Huh?

CHARLIE
You asking me?

BERNARD
Beats me dude.

MELANIE
I haven't a clue.

JANE
What are you talking about?

JAMES
How the hell should I know.

CHARLIE
Damn good question.

MELANIE
It's a mystery to me.

Robert
As DeNiro would day...You talkin to me?

JANE
Who ever knows, really?

BERNARD
Run that by me again.

ROBERT
Go ask your mother...your grandmother!

SANDRA
(concluding)

Elder wisdom ain't what it's cracked up to be, is it? We are all still learning.

JAMES

There's a picture of me holding my 18-month-old son in my arms at the beach on vacation, and we were both in our bathing suits, and I was comforting this sandy child who was obviously in some sort of toddler distress. The picture is one of many on my screen saver, and every time I see it, I dwell on it for as long as I can... thinking, wondering how different things would be now if I could only go back to that time and start again.

CHARLIE

When we start reflecting on our lives what we did and didn't do, what regrets we have and what we would have done differently had we had the chance we can either nose dive into depression and wallow there until we slowly deteriorate into nothing, or we can see the past for what it is when we made choices, decisions; took roads we thought were best, making them on the knowledge and information we had at the time. Turns out some of that knowledge was incomplete made complete only in the living of life over a lifetime, and the information was tainted by others who were also traveling on roads that were decided incorrectly for them.

JAMES

I get that, but either way we have to deal with the oncoming end. Some of us want to live it out no matter what the quality of life, since we are always teachers and learners even in death, and there are reasons for being here until we're not. Others of us want only to end the pain and despair that we feel and that we most likely will cause our loved ones left to take care of us and our disarrayed life. That's when we think about how we will cleverly end it all.

MELANIE

Don't you think we're here to grow together, to mutate, to meld, to mesh into one human race... one in love, in care, in belief, in thought, in word, in deed and in spirit. Then we will be one with the creator... the universal energy that has split us all apart like a big bang to see if and when we will ever find our way back to wholeness.

SANDRA

Or we could just be meant to be a diverse hodge podge of humanity trying to figure it out dealing with all the crap it brings just being here. Who knows? We're just waiting to see.

JANE

Waiting. For what? Lose weight. Feel better. Better time. Miss my show. Too

much. Wrong day. Trouble. Tired. Angry.
Sad. Depressed. Too late. Do it Now...
Don't wait ...could be too late. When you
have nothing to do and it doesn't bother
you, it's hard to find something you want
to do.   Criticize. Easy to do. Hard to
take.

CHARLIE

So much to do. So much to still learn. So
much noise of knowledge. And pressures to
catch up. From outside. Inside. Knowledge
gone wild! Overwhelm! and Exhaustion!
Love my Naps.

JAMES

Paralyzed in memories. Stuck in the past.
Nothing but fear of what's not there.. of
what's not known. What am I going
to do today? Nothing. I've already done
that.

JANE

Skin thins. Wrinkles wrinkle. Get deeper
and multiply. Feet unsure. Slightly now.
Minor bumps. Joints ache. Ears strain
to hear. Eyes squint to see. Teeth turn
colors, if they stay. Gait slows down.
Thinking takes longer. Uncle Sam's meds
arrive. Chairs that lift and sometimes
walkers... things that say Old. How can it
be? My self still here! My heart still
young! Life still full! And ready for
more!

ROBERT

Me, too. I'm ready for more. Been Ready.
I took the less traveled path. No one
knew what they were doing, although
brave. Took the most traveled path... not
many knew there either. Keep guessing.
Keep trying. There might be an answer.
Will? To avoid the stuff that could cut
my life shorter. Will? motivation to do
what I know to do. Can't find it. Where's
will? I've lost will. What else you got?

BERNARD

Well, there's always Anger. Deal with it,
Can't stuff it. It will go somewhere
else...inside...outside...all around. Can't
stay. Has to go. Has to be. How? Where?
When?... are the hard parts.

JAMES

What I owe. What to give back? What?
Nothing. Got nothing, gave nothing.
Dissatisfied. Depressed. Slow death
in place. What's left? Alternative...
Self a mess. Hear the Wake-up call.
Opportunities. Not problems. Find
value. Find purpose. Now's the time.
What we've already done doesn't really
matter anymore. What we have left to do
does. There are things we can do that we
should have already done... And now we
can!!

TRANSITION

Part 7

The Road Most Travel

Knowing that the road
is going to end, and
wondering how we
travel those
last miles.

PART 7
THE ROAD MOST TRAVEL

BERNARD shows and reads final card and

BERNARD
The only way I can make it now, day to day, is to believe that all of it all... everything that happens, the good and the bad are part of the larger picture, the grand design, the ultimate truth, the final secret, the revelation of divine purpose, the coming together of it all as one. Otherwise I would have given up long ago... when it all started seeming too real, unfair, inconsiderate, without purpose, with no meaning and downright hateful! The enormous pain and agony suffered by most of humanity.

SANDRA
What could possibly be the purpose? The world is taught about the love a heavenly father has for his children and it has become more and more difficult to see how that love and our hate, agony, desperate and mean lives could possibly coexist even if a divine all-powerful creator makes it so. I'm feeling it. Thinking it is not knowing it but it does help me better understand and accept and believe but I don't have to like it.

BERNARD

I don't think we're supposed to.

CHARLIE

It's out there. One is waiting for me. Looking to pounce on or in me and take me away. Which one? So many could. No signs yet. Many seeds sowed. Who they were. What they had. What I did. What I did not do. All sets it up. Docs and meds stall it all... one for this, one for that. One will break through. One will take me down. In sleep is best. Oh, when I think of all the damage to lives other than mine, please, god, not a reckless teenage driver.

MELANIE

Best friends come and go. Only the right ones stay. You (to JANE) are one. My best one. Stay.

JANE/MELANIE

(Playfully back and forth)

New best friends. Pharmacists. Receptionists. Appointment makers. Cashiers. Bag boys. Technicians. Mechanics. Handy men. Docs. Nurses. Walkers. Hired Help. Meds... all of them...

(together) Stay!

ROBERT

One. Two. Three docs for me and then four more. Enough! No more! How many do we

need to say what we all know...Well you're
just getting old. Oh, great! How much do
I owe you for that, doc.

We don't know it until we get here... how
life is so short. Now we know to be
selective. Don't waste time with what
we have. Choose carefully. Don't diddle
daddle! Oh, and don't forget to ask your
doctor if you're healthy enough to not
diddle daddle!

JAMES

When her mother was sick and on her way
out she was there, day and night and
in between. Little things. Big things.
Silly things. Serious things. Clean and
dirty things. Holding hands... sharing
tears and memories of mostly good. Loving
dedication to pay back what she got. She
was called The Angel. When she's ready,
who will her angel be? Maybe me.

SANDRA

Thinking of those who have gone before.
Missing some. Ashamed at not missing
others. Parents. Friends. Work mates.
Wives. Husband. Brothers. Sisters. Aunts.
and uncles. Some cousins. So many...
waiting for one of them to tell me what's
next.

JANE

Old folks are slow to panic about dying.
We don't worry too much about that part.

It's the going. The how. The when. The
how long. The what's been. The what's
left.

MELANIE

Friends no more. It's difficult to even
see him now. Where did he go. That guy
I knew disappeared into his anger. His
regrets. His losses. His sadness. And I
can't seem to bring him home.

BERNARD

Getting harder to remember to take all
those pills. Got a daily dose box. Didn't
help. Forgot where I put it. Wondered
if missing days of doses would kill me.
Nope I'm still here. And I'm gonna make
the most of it...let that be the thing that
kills me!!

ROBERT

All the time we hear it. Fixed income.
Tight budget Simplify. Downsize. Next...
all that's left... Lays chips and a walk-
in closet!   What you put in is what you
get out. Heard that baloney. What you put
in is what you put in...what you get back?
Up to you.

MELANIE

Everybody will be telling us what to do!
Our children will want to become our
parents, giving orders, and commands!!
Don't take it! Let 'em have it! Don't
let 'em have it! Stand your ground.

There's a lot to lose. Freedom. Pride.
Checkbook. Keys. Home. Self. Life. Hold
on to what you got. Till you don't.

ROBERT

Last night, like many other nights of
late, in deep dark sleeplessness, replays
of days and years toss and tumble me
inside with frowns mostly. Some smiles.
Regrets and Successes… a few, mostly
gone. Like, up ahead, those who are <u>there</u>
already, "there" meaning almost all gone,
in places where they would rather not be.
What's going on with them? The lives they
live. Their eyes tell so much. And make
me wonder… can I do that? Go there. Be
there.

BERNARD

How to keep going, To not give up, Find
the Spark. Hope. Strength. Courage.
Desire. We have known hard times. Young
ones don't know. Don't want to hear it.
Oh what marvels we could share. Oh what
input to avoid pot holes, walls, ditches,
fires, losses. Grief. Lots of grief. How
do we do it in spite of. That's just us?
That's who we are!

CHARLIE

That's just us. Sounds like a cliché to
me. Clichés. It's never too late. Get a
new lease on life. Everything's gonna
be alright. You're only as young as you
feel. Get up, get going. Don't worry
about it. Help is just around the

corner. Blue skies are up ahead. It's
not the years in your life but the life
in your years. Live every day like it's
your last. It ain't over till it's over.
Helpful? Not a bit. Sometimes it IS over
before it's over. That part. And words
just won't save us.

JAMES

Let's say Tomorrow is the last day,
for everybody. What would you do
today? What would you want today
to be? For me… a soft rain falling
quietly from slightly cooled grey
skies. Scotch on the side table.
Light classical piano music playing
softly. Candles lighting us both in
cozies lying in bed waiting, holding,
remembering. Thankful.

SANDRA

Closets. Attics. Basements. Storage. All
that stuff gathered. Go through it. Clean
it out. Like the clutter in life. Who's
interested? Who cares? Not the kids.
Why put them through it? There are some
things that are hard to trash. Ok with
replacement, some new stuff is fine. But
don't throw out the old. It is us.

(ALL in their chairs and begin rocking
except ROBERT who hangs back and delivers
his last speech…then he heads to chair…

ROBERT

Yes, it is us...we are old or we are going to be...but along the way...we found and we lost. We lost and found... People, Places, Things, Feelings, Ideas, Beliefs, Hopes, Dreams, Realities. We all had those starts and stops along the way, living life on the road most travel, and we are still traveling. Still living life, still taking chances...

MELANIE

Inside and outside chances!

BERNARD

But, it feels good to sit

SANDRA

To rock, to hum, to go numb

CHARLIE

To forget

ROBERT

To wallow

JANE

Use Careful balance action with comfort

JAMES

Rock, but don't rock away.

SONG TO THE TUNE OF LET ME CALL YOU SWEETHEART

(ALL)

```
      YOU CAN CALL US SENIORS
      SINCE THAT'S WHO WE ARE

    STARTS AND STOPS ALONG THE WAY
         STILL ALIVE SO FAR

     TAKING EACH DAY AS IT COMES
        LIVING LIFE SO WELL

SO, YOU CAN CALL US OLD FOLKS (SENIORS)
   BUT WE STILL HAVE MUCH TO TELL.

   (LIGHTS FADE OUT DURING FADE OUT,
 SOMEONE CHANGES SHOW CARD TO SHOW

   "That's It Folks! Thank you.")

         (LIGHTS UP FOR
         CURTAIN CALL)

              END
```

About the Author

JIM R. ROGERS (Playwright/Director/James Lament) shares, as he is looking back from his eighth decade, what he is seeing and hearing and feeling: that the progression to getting old is getting heavier as the monologues move toward the end, but not forgetting hope, that there is still life until there isn't. He wrote *Geriatric Monologues* not as a traditional play, but rather, as dramatic readings to mirror the many and varied emotions that go with aging, meant to inspire, encourage, console, comfort and offer some grins to folks who often don't have a lot to grin about.

Jim grew up in a Norman-Rockwell childhood in Tabor City, NC; after UNC-Chapel Hill, served in the Army in Korea; pursued a career in television and film and advertising in Charlotte, Atlanta, New York, and Los Angeles. Then he returned to his Southern roots for a new career as a Parenting and Family Life Educator, working at Coastal Carolina University for more than a decade until he "retired" to create his own business, *still learning, inc.,* and to begin the writing he hadn't had time for (his first book appeared at age 77; now there are 3!). He is grateful for life with his partner in business and life Sally Z. Hare and their dog TBO in Surfside Beach and is honored to share his words and thoughts.

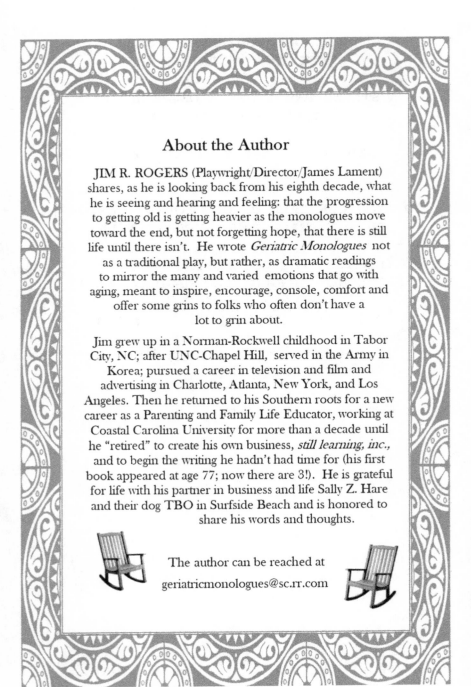

The author can be reached at

geriatricmonologues@sc.rr.com

CPSIA information can be obtained
at www.ICGtesting.com
Printed in the USA
LVHW111040240320
651041LV00002B/495